HOW *NOT* TO PLAY CHESS

By

EUGENE A. ZNOSKO-BOROVSKY

Edited by

FRED REINFELD

DOVER PUBLICATIONS, INC.

NEW YORK

Standard Book Number: 486-20920-2

Manufactured in the United States of America
Dover Publications, Inc.
180 Varick Street
New York, N.Y. 10014

CONTENTS

EDITOR'S INTRODUCTION

How Not to Play Chess has long been regarded as a classic of chess literature. It illustrates Eugene A. Znosko-Borovsky's gift for explaining a difficult subject briefly and yet unhurriedly. Addressed to average players, it imparts valuable knowledge and gives them a glimpse into the delightfully complex problems of master chess.

But this unpretentious book does much more. By defining and illustrating typical chess mistakes, Znosko-Borovsky puts the student on the right road to chess improvement. Though **Znosko-Borovsky** never resorts to a false optimism, he does inspire the reader with confidence in his own ability.

The qualities that distinguish all his books are a clear style, logical reasoning, a contagious love of chess, and a systematic treatment of his subject.

In order to give the reader a chance to get the utmost from **Znosko-Borovsky's** classic, a series of quiz positions have been added. By applying himself to these positions, the student can appraise each situation, examine the possibilities for both sides, prepare a general plan of procedure, and then try to find the concrete sequence that is called for.

He may not always find the best line of play; after all, these examples are from master games. Nevertheless, any reader who makes an honest effort to find the right moves will be richly rewarded when he finally turns to the solutions and sees how a great player met the same difficulties and solved them successfully.

A few words about **Znosko-Borovsky's** playing career may be of interest. He was born at Alexandrovich (Russia) on August 16, 1884 and died on December 31, 1954. He made a name for himself as one of the outstanding Russian masters during the first decade of this century, but during the Revolution he emigrated to France and spent the remaining years of his life in that country.

As a player **Znosko-Borovsky** won some notable individual games from Capablanca, Rubinstein, Tartakover, Euwe, Bogolyubov and other noted masters. But his temperament inclined him more toward analysis than to playing; and it is on his masterly exposition of the game that his fame will securely rest.

Author's Preface

THE title of this little book, and the idea underlying it, came first to my mind in Liverpool, in October, 1926, while walking under the overhead railway and thinking over a lecture which I had been invited to give in that town.

Since that day many years have passed, and more changes have been made in that lecture of mine, which I have since delivered in different languages and in many towns in England, France, and other countries. In the beginning it was planned to take twenty to thirty minutes, but it soon grew longer and sometimes took an hour to an hour and a half to deliver. This lecture I now offer to the kind attention of my readers in an enlarged and revised form.

If the contents of the lecture became larger and richer, its character remained always the same. I sought to find the easiest and most popular form in which to explain certain general ideas of chess strategy, so that even the weakest players could understand me, and those who knew little about chess could follow me without getting tired or bored. I was, therefore, very pleased when I observed that this lecture was everywhere received with great interest and followed with profound attention. If I now publish it in book form, it is because I have very often been asked to do so.

Although this little book is intended for beginners, it makes no claim to be a chess manual. Many things necessary to a beginner are not to be found in it. For instance, I do not explain how the pieces move. Hence, to be able to read and understand the book, the reader must know something about the game. What I do set out to do is to explain certain things that are not usually found in books for beginners, though it is much more necessary that they should be treated there than in books intended for stronger players.

I hope that my explanations will arouse an interest in players, will give them a new love for chess, and will lead them to discover in the game things which perhaps they had never suspected. For I shall never tire of repeating that all study of chess must be based on the following principle :—

Chess is a Game of Understanding,
Not of Memory.

E. A. Z.-B.

Author's Preface to the New Edition

A SKED to revise this book for a new edition, I was inspired in my work by the first advice that I give to my readers—"Avoid Mistakes." Accordingly I tried to find any unhappy expression, any error, however slight, in my text, and to correct them. I tried also to suppress or change every sentence which I felt might lead to confusion or be misunderstood.

Incidentally, I have added three new examples as well as more details in the most difficult part of the book, the analysis of positions, and I hope that now all is clear, and easy to understand. The new diagrams are given in the text as Diagrams A, B, and C.

May my book find in its new form the same or even greater success than was secured by the first edition, may it provide new interest and love for chess, and help amateurs to improve their play.

E. A. Z.-B.

HOW NOT TO
PLAY CHESS

How Not to Play Chess

IN giving my little book its strange title, *HOW NOT TO PLAY CHESS*, I had no desire to be original. So many people, however, try to teach how to play chess, and the results are in general so poor, that it was only natural to seek to attack the problem from the other end. Before trying to teach men how to become saints, is it not well to show them how to avoid sin ?

Perhaps, when you have finished reading this book, you may tell me that I, like so many others, have, after all, taught *how* to play chess. That, however, is my aim in this book. There are many mistakes which you must avoid, if you are to play chess well. Every piece of negative advice which I give must therefore lead to a positive conclusion.

Avoid Mistakes. To avoid mistakes is the beginning, as it is the end, of mastery in chess. If you make no mistakes you can be certain of never losing a game, and very constantly you will win it. And how difficult this is ! Even the strongest masters cannot avoid them. How many games have been lost only because of them ? Tchigorin overlooked a mate in two in the final game of his second match against Steinitz for the world championship and thus lost the match ! ! Here is a position from the game Rosselli *v.* Alekhin, from the recent tournament at Folkestone, which was really a "game of errors."

White here won a P by 28 R × R, P × R; 29 Kt × P on which Black answered P—B6 ? ? and after

DIAGRAM "A"

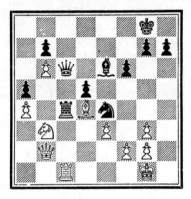

30 Q—B2 White was content to come out one
Pawn minus but with Bishops of opposite colours.
As a matter of fact White could simply win another
P by 30 Kt × Q, P × Q ; 31 B × KtP, because Black
could not play P × Kt, for if so then 32 P—Kt7 and
queens the next move.

But the man is not a machine and in the heat
of battle and under the pressure of the clock even
the champion of the world may make mistakes.
Less pardonable are obvious mistakes in simple positions, especially in the beginning of the game, which
is now so carefully analysed.   One despairs when one
thinks of all the effort expended on the study of
chess, and of the poverty of the results.   Year after
year the same elementary mistakes are repeated, the
same antediluvian traps claim their victims.   It is
almost incredible, yet so it is, and all that the masters
may teach or practise does not seem to help the
amateur in his play one whit.   I will give an example
of an error which is continually being committed.

After the moves 1 P—K4, P—K4 ; 2 Kt—KB3,
Kt—QB3 ; 3 B—B4, P—Q3 ; 4 P—Q4, P—KR3 ;

5 Kt—QB3, B—Kt5 ? ; 6 P×P, Kt×P ? we arrive
at the position shown on Diagram 1.

DIAGRAM 1

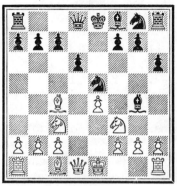

In this position White plays 7 Kt×Kt, offering the
sacrifice of the Q, and after 7 ......, B×Q, mates
in two moves by 8 B×Pch., K—K2 ; 9 Kt—Q5 mate.
(It will be obvious that if Black does not accept the
sacrifice of the Q, but makes any other move, e.g.,
7 ......, P×Kt, White with 8 Q×B has won a
pawn.)

This, the "Blackburne Trap," so called because
that master used to catch three or four of his opponents a night with it, and was really the first to
popularise it, was first brought off by M. de Kermar,
Sir de Légal, Philidor's teacher, in 1702 ! It has
been published in one of its many forms scores of
times. The former Russian champion, M. J.
Tchigorin, was actually caught by a variant of it in
his match with Dr. S. Tarrasch, in 1893, in the
position resulting from the following moves : 1 P—
K4, P—K4 ; 2 Kt—KB3, Kt—QB3 ; 3 B—Kt5,
P—QR3 ; 4 B—R4, Kt—KB3 ; 5 Kt—QB3, B—
QKt5 ; 6 Kt—Q5, B—R4 ; 7 O—O, P—QKt4 ;

8 B—Kt3, P—Q3 ; 9 P—Q3, B—KKt5 ; 10 P—QB3, Kt—K2 ? ? 11 Kt×KP ! Tchigorin was too great a player blindly to take the offered Q, which would lead to mate in three moves, or loss of material and decisive positional disadvantage, but his game was hopeless nevertheless. This example is given to show that the famous trap may crop up in many ways. For instance 1 P—K4, P—K4 ; 2 P—KB4, P—Q3 ; 3 Kt—KB3, Kt—QB3 ; 4 B—B4, B—Kt5 ; 5 Kt—B3, Kt—Q5 ; 6 Kt×KP, B×Q ; 7 B×Pch., etc. It is probably—it should be—the best known of all chess traps, and one would imagine that it was familiar to every player. If you have once really understood, you need never be caught by it. Yet it is constantly recurring : in fact there are few simultaneous displays in which one or more games are not won by it.

What must we infer from this ? That many amateurs have never seen or heard of this trap ? Probably most know it or have been shown it, but they have forgotten all about it, because they never made the principle underlying it their own, nor imagined that it could ever be brought off against them, never really understood it, and so failed to recognise it in another context. The importance of a combination such as this had never been properly explained to them. The combination is only made possible by the cramped position of Black's K, which allows White, at the cost of his Q, to launch a violent attack leading to mate, or the recovery with interest of the material sacrificed plus great positional advantage. In the first example quoted, White nets a whole piece, if Black does not submit to a mate ; in the second, if the Q is taken, after 12 Kt×Ktch., K—B1 (if P×Kt ; 13 B×Pch., K—B1 ; 14 B—R6

mate) ; 13 either Kt—Q7ch., Q × Kt ; 14 Kt × Qch.,
K—K1 ; 15 R × B, K × Kt ; 16 B × P, White's
winning advantage is clear.

I give a further example of another mistake to
show that I have not in the above taken an excep-
tional case. One would imagine that every chess
player must know the brilliant game of Morphy's
which he won in Paris, in 1858, during a performance
at the Opera of *"The Barber of Seville." It has
perhaps been more often published than any other
game.

White : Paul Morphy.

Black : The Duke of Brunswick and Count
Isouard.

1.	P—K4	P—K4
2.	Kt—KB3	P—Q3
3.	P—Q4	B—KKt5 ?
4.	P × P	B × Kt
5.	Q × B	P × P
6.	B—QB4	Kt—KB3
7.	Q—QKt3	Q—K2
8.	Kt—QB3	P—QB3
9.	B—KKt5	P—QKt4

See Diagram 2. In this position Morphy brought
off the following beautiful combination :

10.	K × KtP	P × Kt
11.	B × KtPch.	QKt—Q2
12.	O—O—O	R—Q1
13.	R × Kt !	. . . . . .

Maintaining the pin.

---

* The author gives "Norma" as the Opera in progress, but
Mr. Sergeant gives "The Barber of Seville."

DIAGRAM 2

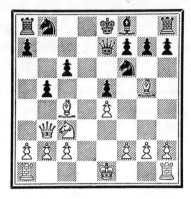

13.	......	R × R
14.	R—Q1	Q—K3
15.	B × Rch.	Kt × B
16.	Q—Kt8ch.	Kt × Q
17.	R—Q 8 mate.	

Black's first mistake is on his third move, which would lead, even if it were not followed by other errors; to an inferior game in any case. Morphy's combination is so beautiful and so well known that such an error should never be repeated. Yet it is being committed over and over again. How many times have I not myself had the opportunity of playing this combination in simultaneous displays! Indeed I once saw almost the whole of Morphy's game repeated by a master, whose opponent was by no means a very weak beginner.

Again, how must we explain this? It is difficult to suppose that these players have never seen this game of Morphy's. They must have seen it several times, for there is hardly a book on chess which does not reproduce it. They have seen it, but they have forgotten it.   They may have been asked to remember it, they were not made to understand the reasons which justified Morphy's combination.   What were the reasons ?   White has four pieces beautifully in play converging on Black's cramped King's position with a fifth, the QR, which can at once be brought up in support.   Against these Black has only two pieces developed, and of these one, the Kt, is pinned, while the Q obstructs her own KB.   This is all the result of Black's early mistakes, such as 3 ......, B—Kt5 ; 6 ......, Kt—KB3 ; 7 ......, Q—K2 ; and especially of 9 ......, P—QKt4, all of which merely served to develop White and bring embarrassment on himself as the sequel showed.   The sacrifice of the Kt, clearing all avenues of approach to the helpless enemy King, is therefore fully justified. Admire the final position in which White has only two pieces left, just enough to give mate and in exactly the same time two of Black's pieces have not even moved.   Note White's 13 R × Kt !, maintaining the pin and hence keeping up the tension until the KR is brought into action.   Had he played 13 B × Kt ch., Black would have been out of half his troubles.   The number of won games thrown away by needlessly or prematurely relieving the enemy from the tension of a pin is legion.

It is better to understand a combination, the principles underlying it, than to memorize it. Analogous combinations may be possible in other positions, after other opening moves.   Provided you have an understanding of the combination, you can take advantage of the position, or avoid the danger, even if you have forgotten the game.   If you have only learnt it by heart, nothing can help you, if you forget it.

Do not make the opening moves automatically and without reflection.

I think that there are several reasons for these mistakes. The first is that amateurs often make the opening moves quite automatically, without thinking of their meaning. They have seen them made in many master games; they repeat them as being good moves, but without understanding the idea which is behind them, their possible weaknesses or dangers, or what they may threaten ; so that if their opponent make some unfamiliar move, possibly a very weak one, they are at once at sea, and know not how to reply to it, or take advantage of it. It is impossible to remember all the variations and sub-variations in an opening, but if you really understand the main line of play, if you have grasped the spirit of the opening, you will seldom be at a loss for a good reply to an unfamiliar move of your opponent's.

All amateurs know the following initial moves in the QP Opening, which is now so popular : 1 P—Q4, P—Q4 ; 2 P—QB4, P—K3 ; 3 Kt—QB3, Kt—KB3 ; 4 B—Kt5, and they have many times seen Black play here 4 ......, B—K2 or QKt—Q2. They know that those moves are made by the great masters, and therefore repeat them, without thinking about their meaning. They have no idea, for instance, that with 4 ......, QKt—Q2, Black sets a pretty trap, which may lead to a fine combination. The position is that given in Diagram 3.

A glance shows us that in this position White can win a P, because with his KKt pinned, Black's QP is insufficiently protected. Is this an oversight on Black's part ? Cannot White safely play 5 P×P, P×P ; 6 Kt×P ? I am convinced that the majority of weak amateurs, playing together, would not

DIAGRAM 3

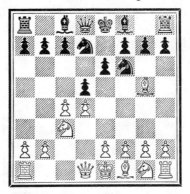

understand the issue. White would not see that he
could win a P. Nor Black that his P was in danger.
Moreover, I am equally sure that if White did play
P × P, Black would not find the right reply, and
would blame the Masters for leading him astray.

I said that with 4 . . . . . . , QKt—Q2, Black was
really laying a pretty trap, for after 5 P × P, P × P ;
6 Kt × P, Black plays 6 . . . . . . , Kt × Kt, giving up
his Q ! But after 7 B × Q, B—Kt5 ch., White has no
option, he must interpose his Q, so 8 Q—Q2, B × Q
ch. ; 9 K × B, K × B, and Black, having regained his
sacrificed Q, is a whole piece up. I would wager that
ninety-nine out of every hundred players in making
the move 4 . . . . . . , QKt—Q2, do not realise that
they are offering to sacrifice their Q, and they would
be greatly astonished if anyone told them that this
was the case.

A very similar combination occurs in the following variation in the Centre Counter Game : 1 P—
K4, P—Q4 ; 2 P × P, Q × P ; 3 Kt—QB3, Q—Q1 ;
4 P—Q4, Kt—QB3 ; 5 Kt—KB3, B—Kt5 ; 6 P—
Q5, Kt—K4 ? ; 7 Kt × Kt !, B × Q ; 8 B—QKt5 ch.,

P—B3 ; 9 P×P and wins. This simple combination
which sometimes is no more than a trap can often
become a very complicated one and then even great
Masters fall.

DIAGRAM "B"

Diagram "B" shows a position from a tournament
game between Rubinstein and Duras. The latter
played here 1 ......, P—QKt4, giving White the
opportunity of bringing off the splendid combination
which follows : 2 QKt—K5, Kt×Kt ; 3 Kt×Kt ! !
B×Q ; 4 B×P ch., Kt—Q2 ; 5 B×Kt ch., Q×B ;
6 Kt×Q, B—R4 ; 7 Kt—K5 and wins.   If 4
......, K—Q1, then 5 R×B ch., K—B1 ; 6 B—
R6 ch. Wins. If the fact that even Masters occa-
sionally overlook such combinations consoles us,
good ! ! but it must not be allowed to discourage us
or induce us to imagine that our continued studies
would be of no avail. On the contrary we must
understand that such cases are rare exceptions in
master practice, and that must give us the courage
and the desire to do better, to become at least the
equal of the Masters.

Do not memorise variations, try to understand them. There is another reason for these mistakes, and an important one. In my experience the majority of books on the openings are concerned more with giving numberless variations than with giving such explanations of the game as would lead the beginner really to understand the why and the wherefore of the moves he sees made ; and in this way encourage the development of his Chess sense, thus enabling him to think his own thoughts in Chess, based as they will then be on the wide principles underlying the game. As it is, the reader, after wading through these endless variations, has probably really understood but a very small number of the moves given. He sets out to memorise the variations. And what will be the result ? There can be only one. In a couple of weeks most of these variations will have been entirely forgotten ; the moves which he does succeed in remembering will have probably got into their wrong order, or otherwise be confused in his mind. As he never really understood them, he remembers only that such-and-such moves are made in a given opening, and the odds are on his making them at the wrong moment, or in the wrong variation.

An admirable example of the danger of confusing two variations in the opening appears in the following little game from a simultaneous display given by Nimzowitsch in 1920 : 1 P—K4, P—K4 ; 2 Kt—KB3, Kt—QB3 ; 3 B—Kt5, Kt—B3 ; 4 O—O, P—Q3 ; 5 P—Q4, Kt×P ? Black must play here B—Q2. He has confused, or tried to combine, two perfectly good defences to the Ruy Lopez, the Berlin Defence, 3 ......, Kt—KB3 followed after 4 O—O by Kt×P, and the Steinitz Defence, 3 ......,

P—Q3. By playing 4 ......, P—Q3, he passes over to this defence, and if he had understood the idea of it, in fact the idea of either of these defences, he would never have dreamt of playing 5 ......, Kt×P. Punishment follows with great swiftness. 6 P—Q5, P—QR3 ; 7 B—Q3, Kt—B3 ; 8 P×Kt, P—K5 ; 9 R—K1, P—Q4 ; 10 B—K2 ! ! P×Kt. Black is unconscious of his doom. 11 P×KtP ! B×P ; 12 B—QKt5 mate. A pretty aspect of the combination lies in the fact that if instead of B×P Black plays 11 ......, P×B ; 12 P×R=Q, and Black cannot take White's Q at Q1 as his P is pinned. Instances of confusion such as this abound.

Again, a strange move by his opponent will throw him entirely out of gear, and even if the moves on both sides are all made "according to book," there comes a time when he is thrown on his own resources. The variation he has learnt closes, perhaps, with the words, "White has the better game." That is all very well, but what on earth is he to do with this "better game" ? How is he to turn his superior position to account ? To the solution of this problem the book does not offer him any help.

Is it surprising that many who have a real desire to learn chess give up the study of the game in the face of such disappointing experiences, as too difficult, or go on "wood shifting," neither knowing nor caring anything about theory ? Our task, therefore, is clear. We must seek to remove the difficulties, and to convince the reader that there is such a thing as "chess made easy."

You must not, however, imagine that you will be able to play a good game of chess by the light of your native understanding alone. In every art or science we have to build upon the work of our

predecessors.   So, too, in chess we have to know
something about the openings and the pitfalls they
contain.   Some of the traps and combinations in the
openings are so complicated that it is easier to
remember how they run than to work them out
during the game.   Nor would the average amateur
of moderate skill in general be capable of doing so.
An instance is the following pretty combination in
the Ruy Lopez known as the Tarrasch Trap.   Over
55 years ago, in 1891, in the February number of the
Deutsche Schachzeitung, Dr. Tarrasch published the
trap to expose a danger lying in wait for the unwary
in the Steinitz Defence to the Ruy Lopez.   In the
following year at the Dresden Tournament of 1892,
Dr. Tarrasch in his game against the master, G.
Marco, was able to repeat the whole combination !
No one to-day, after all those years, who pretends
to be a serious chess player should be ignorant of it,
yet it, too, claims its regular victims.   The game
runs thus : 1 P—K4, P—K4 ; 2 Kt—KB3, Kt—
QB3 ; 3 B—Kt5, P—Q3 ; 4 P—Q4, B—Q2 ; 5 O—O,
Kt—B3 ; 6 R—K1, B—K2 ; 7 Kt—B3.   See Diagram 4.   White's last move looks innocent enough,
for it seems to leave the position in the centre
essentially unchanged.   This, however, is far from
being the case, and if Black continues his normal
development with 7 ......, O—O, he will at
best lose a P, if he sees what is coming in time,
more probably, however, a piece or the exchange.
This is because White's KP is now, after Kt—
QB3, doubly protected.   Marco played unsuspect-
ingly 7 ......, O—O ; and the game proceeded :
8 B×Kt, B×B (If 8 ......, P×B ; Black after
9 P×P, P×P ; 10 Kt×P will have lost a valuable
centre P, without any compensation whatever.

DIAGRAM 4

However, this would be the lesser evil) ; 9 P×P,
P×P ; 10 Q×Q, QR×Q ; 11 Kt×P, B×P ; 12
Kt×B, Kt×Kt ; 13 Kt—Q3, P—KB4 ; 14 P—KB3,
B—B4 ch. ; 15 Kt×B, Kt×Kt ; 16 B—Kt5 !, R—
Q4 ; 17 B—K7 !, R—K1 ; 18 P—QB4 and wins, for
a piece or the exchange is lost. If instead of 10
. . . . . ., QR×Q Black had played KR×Q the result
would have been the same, for again after 11 Kt×P,
B×P ; 12 Kt×B, Kt×Kt ; 13 Kt—Q3, P—KB4 ;
14 P—KB3, B—B4 ch. ; 15 K—B1 !, Black must lose
a piece or the exchange. Note that if in the first
variation where Black plays 10 . . . . . ., QR×Q, the
White K, on being checked by the B, move to B1 as
he did in the second, Black would get off scot free,
for he could play 15 . . . . . ., B—Kt3, and after 16
P×Kt, P×P ch. recovers the piece. The meaning
of the trap is easy of explanation. Easier still is it
to remember that the moment White's KP in this
variation is twice protected, Black must play P×P
at once and then go on with his development.

Do not believe all that you are told. Examine, verify, use your reason.

It must not be thought that it is always easy to give an explanation on some point in chess which shall satisfy the enquirer. For instance, I remember well the astonishment of one who asked me : "Is it true that in the opening it is not good to move the same piece several times ?" "Quite true," I replied. "Is it true," he then asked, "that the Ruy Lopez is one of the best openings ?" "Yes, it is," I agreed. "But how can that be," he objected, "when in the Ruy Lopez White makes four of his first nine moves with his KB ?" He was quite right, for the opening moves are : 1 P—K4, P—K4 ; 2 Kt—KB3, Kt—QB3 ; 3 *B—Kt*5, P—QR3 ; 4 *B—R*4, Kt—B3 ; 5 O—O, B—K2 ; 6 R—K1, P—QKt4 ; 7 *B—Kt*3, P—Q3 ; 8 P—QB3, Kt—QR4 ; 9 *B—B*2, O—O, etc., and one had to explain that to bring this result about Black has had to weaken his Q side by his pawn moves, that he has himself moved his QKt twice, and on to a bad square at R4, and that in general if your opponent plays correctly, it is impossible to obtain something for nothing !

This shows how difficult it often is to explain the game to a beginner, so that it is hardly to be wondered at that many manuals refrain from any attempt to do so. The simplest rules are subject to many exceptions, and even one that is fundamental may, in certain cases, find itself in contradiction with others. Moreover, the explanations which are often given can hardly satisfy even the weakest player. Thus, after 1 P—K4, P—K4 ; 2 Kt—KB3, it is usually said that White's second move was made with the idea of winning Black's KP. Yet this cannot possibly be the true explanation of the move, for even if Black does nothing, White cannot win the P, thus : 3 Kt×P, Q—K2 ; 4 Kt—KB3, Q×P ch. Confusion of ideas and misunderstanding of this kind must be avoided. The Kt attacks the P, he threatens to take it, he does not at the moment threaten to win it. If he ever does, it will only be owing to bad play on Black's part. The true idea of 2 Kt—KB3 is, as will be seen later, to get a grip on the centre squares, Q4, K5.

In Chess, as in other things, it is best to proceed from the simple to the complex, and in a natural order. This is the easier in Chess as we can clearly distinguish three parts of the game.

The game of Chess is based on mechanical, or mathematical laws, which can be learnt by anyone. They present no difficulty whatever, and there is really nothing of Chess, properly speaking, in them. Their importance lies in the fact that they are above discussion, they are independent of any personal taste or opinion, they do not change with the time nor under the influence of different schools or temperaments. They must be conformed to by everyone, whether he be a great master or a tyro. These laws form the basement of our Chess structure.

On the ground floor we find the struggle of Chess ideas, and here it is that we first meet what we call Chess. No special gifts are needed to understand them, for they are quite logical. All that is required is that we should hold fast to the logic of them, not become illogical in our application of them. But in Chess, as in life, it would seem to be a most difficult thing to be logical !

And lastly, on the first and best floor of our Chess building, are lodged the individual gift for making combinations, and the capacity to understand a position. This last is the most difficult thing in Chess, and is the property of only the strongest Masters. It is an individual thing, almost impossible to teach, yet even in this branch of Chess we can help the student on his way, since the understanding of a position, positional sense, is based on what we can learn in the other two storeys of our Chess edifice. He who has really learnt the lessons there contained will be able to appreciate a position rightly, not perhaps in such detail or so quickly as a Master would, but nevertheless well enough to enable him to defend his game. As to combinations, no one assuredly can invent them, if he have no imagination, but here too, we can help the student by pointing out the conditions under which different combinations are possible, and also the relations which exist between them and the positions out of which they may arise.

In this little book, which is addressed to beginners, we shall have to leave these difficult questions aside, and confine ourselves to the primary elements of the game, which it is essential that they should master.

However, you must not think that there is anything extremely difficult even in these examples of the highest Chess inspiration. The great privilege of our game is that there is nothing hidden ; everyone can see all that is on the chessboard, and, what is more, no piece can remain unnoticed. It is necessary only to be able to see, and the elements of Chess are so united, the mechanical laws are so intimately

united with the highest Chess ideas that these appear
no more than the logical results of what the primary
elements indicate. The trouble is generally that
inexperienced people have no real Chess ideas. What
must they seek ? For what must they play ? I have
not the space to explain fully what I mean by "Chess
ideas," but the examples given in this book must do
this for me. I will only point out here that most of
them have a purely mechanical foundation. Take,
for instance, an open line and the necessity of open
lines for our pieces. That is a pure Chess idea, but
at the same time quite a mechanical conception.
Take the necessity to create a weak square in the
opponent's camp and to occupy it with a piece of
our own. Is that not also purely mechanical ? And
so on. Therefore the finest combinations have a
mechanical foundation and so soon as this is easily
seen and recognised, everyone becomes able to find
brilliant combinations.

Look, for instance, at the Diagram "C." It is
a position which occurred in a game between Forgacs
and Tartakower at the International Tournament at

DIAGRAM "C"

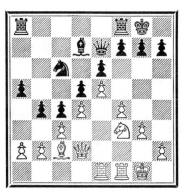

two squares. At Kt2 he has four moves, to R4, B4, K3 and K1. At B2, again, he will have six moves, to R1, R3, Kt4, K4, Q3, Q1. If, however, he is on a centre square he will with eight moves command eight squares. From this it is obvious that the Kt becomes stronger as he approaches the centre. The same is true of all pieces, so that he whose pieces command the centre has the advantage over his opponent.

It follows from this that the strength of each piece varies according to its position. Hence the accepted relative values of the pieces—Q = 10, R = 5, B or Kt = 3, etc., only express their mean values. In reality, the value of a piece is continually changing, and to estimate the true values of our pieces at any moment, we have to analyse the position. Later we shall see on what depends the strength of the various pieces ; for the present it is enough to know that they increase in strength as they approach the centre. Since, therefore, our aim must be to make our pieces converge on the centre, the proper tactics to be followed in the openings are clear : advance of the centre pawns, and occupation, or control, of central points by pieces.

Do not abandon the centre to your adversary. You will now, I hope, not ask, as many amateurs do, why your first move should not be the advance of one of your Rook pawns, nor whether, if you make such a first move, your game is necessarily lost. There is no forced win in sight, but your move had no sense, and if your opponent ultimately wins the game through having developed his game centrally, with corresponding increase in the strength of his pieces, you must not be surprised if you are punished for not pursuing similar tactics.

The immense importance attached to the control of the centre is shown in the so-called hyper-modern openings and systems, with the fianchetto of the B's, which have been devised with this fundamental idea in view. The B's posted at Kt2 occupy the long diagonals which pass through the centre. They therefore hold the centre, though from a distance, supporting your grip on it, attacking the enemy's. And here it should be noted that to hold the centre, it is not always necessary to post pieces there ; it is sufficient that the centre should come under the direct fire of your pieces, so that the enemy may be prevented or hindered from establishing his pieces there. It will also be obvious that if you occupy the centre squares with your pieces prematurely, that is without proper preparation, they will likely be exchanged, or driven off by the enemy, and you will have wasted valuable time. A preliminary preparation is therefore indicated. Hence the fianchetto development of the B's, bearing on the centre, just referred to.

Do not give up open lines, seize them and hold them. A glance at the board shows that the squares form lines which may be vertical, horizontal, or diagonal. These lines are referred to as files, ranks (or rows), and diagonals, respectively. It will be obvious that the longer the lines are, the stronger will they be. Those lines which pass through the vitally important centre squares are also stronger than those on the flanks of the board. It is therefore important to seize and hold strong lines with pieces which act along them. Neither a P nor a Kt can control a line ; for the former threatens, i.e., holds, only two squares, the latter, though he may threaten eight squares, yet can hold only two on any given line. With a R or a B (and, of course, a Q) it is different, and it is very important to get open lines for your R's and B's to operate on, files for the R's, diagonals for the B's.

And certainly such lines must be open. If, for instance, a B be on a diagonal which is occupied by pieces, or, worse, by blocked pawns, i.e., pawns which cannot move, his strength will be very small, and will only increase as these obstacles to his action are removed. The same is true of R's on files. The importance of opening lines for your B's and R's is therefore clear. It follows that if, say, both you and your opponent have a R, that R will be the stronger which is on an open file. If both are on open files, that R will in general be the stronger which is on the stronger, i.e., more central file. You will understand now why it is that players will struggle desperately to get control of open lines (files or diagonals). It is to add strength to their pieces. Of course, if a combination is possible leading to a clear win, you need not think of such things as opening lines, just as you would not postpone giving mate in order to capture a P which was en prise ! When, however, there is no clear forced win in sight, then you must do all that you possibly can to strengthen your pieces, i.e., your position, which you can best do by getting control of as many squares on the board as possible.

You will have seen that by simply examining the board we have been able to reach several very important conclusions, which indeed form the bases of all Chess strategy ; and you must agree that it has been very simple to arrive at them, and that no

special gift for the game was required to understand
them. It will also not be very difficult now to
establish at any given moment which side is the
stronger ; for superiority in any position depends on
the position of every piece engaged.

Do not create
weak points in
your game for the
enemy to seize.
We know that while the Chess
men differ in strength, the weakest of them all is the P. This
very weakness is sometimes a
great strength ; for if it attack a
piece, that piece must retire, since
in general it would be disastrous to exchange a piece
for a pawn. If, therefore, you place a piece on a
square which can be attacked by an enemy pawn,
that piece can never feel quite secure, and you
cannot say that you really occupy the square. You
are only doing so on sufferance, so to speak. A
square can only be said to be occupied when it
cannot be attacked by a pawn. Such a square will
be weak and a source of danger to the player in
whose camp it is, and, conversely, a potential strong
point for his opponent. If therefore you see such a
weak square in your opponent's position, you must
try to occupy it with one of your pieces or pawns,
and the nearer that square is to his base, the more
dangerous will the occupation be to him. The great
Steinitz used to say that if he could establish a Kt
at his K6 or Q6, he could then safely go to sleep,
for the game would win itself. And even on the
5th rank, a Kt at K5, say, threatens at once four
important squares in the enemy camp, QB6, Q7,
KB7, and KKt6, and seriously cramps the freedom
of his pieces. Again, a P which has arrived at K6
not only threatens the squares Q7 and KB7, but

also cuts the whole enemy position in two, often with disastrous effects to him.

The pawn configuration forms the skeleton of the position, and since a pawn can only move forward, it follows that as a pawn advances, weak squares are left on its flank and rear, for these can no longer be threatened or protected by the pawn. We call "holes" squares in the pawn position which cannot be defended by pawns. For instance, in the configuration PKR3, PKKt2, PKB3, there is a hole at KKt3. Such holes must be especially watched, and if possible controlled by pieces.

After what has been said I think you will now understand how a square which we should unhesitatingly call a strong square on an empty board, e.g., the square QB5, may from your point of view be less strong or actually weak, when pieces are on the board. This will be the case if your piece occupying that square has less effective strength than it would have elsewhere, or from where it has no liaison with your other pieces. This does not mean that the theory is wrong, but that you have played unwisely in moving your piece to that square.

Do not lose time. There is another element in Chess of which we have not yet spoken, and that is time. In Chess we play with men which act in time (i.e., moves) as well as in space (i.e., the board). Just as you can get an advantage in space by occupying or controlling strong points, so too you can get an advantage in time, gain a tempo (or tempi), as it is called, if you are earlier in completing your development than your opponent, or press home your attack quicker. If you have played, say, B—Kt5, and afterwards retire it to B4, you will, *ceteris paribus,* have lost a move ; for you have done in two moves what could have been done in one. If in the meanwhile your opponent has made two good moves, he will have gained an advantage over you in time, will in fact have gained a tempo. In this case, thus put, the loss in time is obvious, but very often several moves will have intervened between the two moves of the B, and the loss in time, though as real, will escape the notice of the player. Again, ill-considered exchanges provide fine examples of time wasting. For instance, if you exchange a piece which has made one or more moves for an undeveloped enemy piece, you lose the whole of the tempi consumed by your piece, and the same is true if you exchange a piece which has moved several times for an enemy piece which has only moved once, or when your opponent can make the recapture with a piece hitherto undeveloped. And it must be remembered that the loss of a single tempo may lead to the ultimate loss of the game, since you have given your opponent time which you may never be able to retrieve, with the consequence that he will be before you in developing his attack.

You may ask, how can one know at any given moment who has the advantage in time, which side has gained or lost tempi. Very simply. If you want to know which side has the advantage in material, you count the forces left on the board ; to ascertain the advantage in space you count the strong points held or controlled by the two opponents. So, too, in time, you must count the useful moves made by both players to determine whether one has gained tempi from the other.

As a concrete example, we will take the opening moves in one of the main variations of the Ruy

Lopez : 1 P—K4, P—K4 ; 2 Kt—KB3, Kt—QB3 ;
3 B—Kt5, P—QR3 ; 4 B—R4, Kt—KB3 ; 5 O—O,
Kt×P ; 6 P—Q4, P—QKt4 ; 7 B—Kt3, P—Q4 ;
8 P×P, B—K3 ; 9 P—QB3, B—K2. To ascertain
whether there have been any tempi lost on either
side, we must, by counting, calculate in how few
moves the position could be reached by each party.
White could have arrived at his position with 3 P
moves, 2 B moves, 1 Kt move, castling 1 move : in
all 7 moves ; Black with 3 P moves, 2 B moves, 3 Kt
moves, or 8 moves in all. From this we see that
since both sides have actually made 9 moves, White
has lost a tempo, since he took 9 moves to reach a
position which could have been arrived at in 7, as
compared with 8 made by Black. Black has therefore gained in time. Whether White has not compensation in Black's weakened Q's side which has
been to a certain extent compromised by the advance
of the P's is another matter. For the moment we
are only concerned with the calculation of the tempi
gained or lost.

To show what loss in time can mean in the
opening a flagrant case may be quoted, taken from
a game between two Masters in an important
tournament.

1 P—QB4, Kt—KB3 ; 2 Kt—QB3, P—K3 ;
3 P—K4, B—Kt5 ; 4 P—K5, Kt—Kt1 (forced,
for if 4 ......, B×Kt ; 5 QP×B, Kt—K5 ; 6 Q—
Kt4 wins the piece, or extracts a heavier penalty),
5 Q—Kt4, B—B1, and Black has lost 4 tempi. An
amazing position ! See Diagram 5. You will not
be surprised to learn that Black died under extreme
torture. Here the issue is not confused by any
counter-balancing advantages. Such a case is rare.
As a rule, if both sides have played correctly as in

DIAGRAM 5

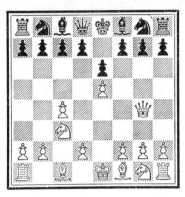

the Ruy Lopez example discussed above, one side or the other may have gained a tempo, but has had to give his opponent something for it. Remembering that the time element, though an important one, does not stand alone. It is only one of three which enter into our mechanical analysis of a position.

Unless you analyse the position you will achieve nothing. We have just made a mechanical or exterior analysis of the position, and I can hear you asking : Is it really necessary to make such an analysis, and if so, why ? The answer is that it is indispensable. In order to determine on your proper course, it is essential that you should know exactly how you stand. How often have I heard players say : I knew that I had the better position, but I did not know what to do to take advantage of it ; I made some bad moves and lost the game. I would then always ask them : Did you really analyse the position ? Did you know in what precisely your advantage consisted ? If you had done so, you would have known what to do, and you would not have lost your game.

You see, it is not enough merely to have the feeling that you stand better or worse than your opponent ; you must know and understand exactly in what consists this superiority or inferiority. If you have the better position you can take the initiative and attack. If your opponent has the advantage in position, you must concentrate on defence. If your advantage is very great, attack vigorously ; if it be only small, be prudent, play carefully, do not attempt to hasten things. Only a thorough analysis of the position can guide you to your proper path.

The complete analysis of a position is a long and difficult task. You should always begin with a mechanical or exterior analysis, of which the result must always be the same whoever makes it, since it depends neither on the taste nor the opinions of the player. Examine everything that is on the board, note those pieces which are well or ill placed, you will then see whose pieces are the most effective and therefore stronger, yours or your opponent's. Next estimate the strength or weakness of the various squares : the result will show you which has the advantage in space. Lastly, examine the time element to ascertain whether either side has gained tempi over the other. If, as a result of your analysis, you find that you hold the advantage in all three elements, you need not trouble, and you may play to win. If, however, your opponent holds the advantage in all or some of these elements, there is something wrong with your position, you must play circumspectly, and endeavour to rectify what is amiss.

A thorough analysis of this kind can, of course, be made at any moment of the game, but as it takes time, you will certainly not repeat it, unless it be necessary. It often happens that a player with the better game begins an attack and continues with it, when the superiority in position which perhaps justified it has vanished. He may not have made the strongest moves, or his opponent may have discovered a resource which he had not anticipated, the bearing of which he perhaps does not quite grasp. Whatever it be, his positional advantage has disappeared, and with it all reason for continuing the attack. This, however, he does not observe, and goes on attacking as vigorously, with the result that his attack is thrown back, his position crumples up, and he loses a game which he had thought himself certain to win. He cannot understand how this could have happened. Yet a careful analysis of the position at the proper moment would have warned him of his danger, and the result might have been very different.

Now that you have thoroughly understood how important it is to analyse the position, I can, without any fear of discouraging you, point out that the "exterior" analysis, which we have been considering, is only the first part of a complete analysis. Having made it, we must then pass on to the dynamic or interior analysis of the position.

Suppose that you have advanced your RP to the 5th rank, and that in doing so you have gained one or more tempi. If this pawn thus advanced be now weak, your gain in time is illusory, being out-balanced by your loss in strength due to the weakness of this pawn. Again, the fact that your pieces occupied strong points in the enemy camp would profit you little if meantime he mated you in another part of the board. So, too, of what use to

you is the gain of an enemy piece, if in compensation
for its loss he is able to open an irresistible attack on
your position ? This does not mean that your
mechanical analysis was wrong or useless ; far from
it. It means that you must supplement it by a
dynamic or interior analysis, by which you must
seek to ascertain the true balance of values in this
position, in time, space, and material. This will be
not quite so easy to carry out ; but if this first or
mechanical part has been properly done, the dynamic
analysis will not be so very difficult.

Do not leave any piece where it has no range of action or is out of touch with your other pieces. In this analysis your primary
object is to see whether your
pieces have a future, whether
from where they stand they
can occupy stronger squares or
seize, or control, important
files or diagonals. Although
apparently strongly placed, a piece may yet have
no future where it is, since there is no way for it to
occupy, if need be, other perhaps more important
points, or to co-operate effectively with your other
pieces. The value of such a piece, where it is, is
very small. Liaison must be maintained between
your pieces, so that they may co-operate whether
for attack or defence. An isolated piece, out of
contact with his fellows, and therefore unable to
come to their support in time, may well lead to the
loss of the game. Hence the vital importance of
this "interior" analysis of the position. If all is
not well in your camp, if one or more of your pieces
have no "future," or if between your pieces there is
no proper liaison, your course is obvious : put your
house in order while there is yet time. To do this
under enemy fire is not always easy, but the attempt

must be made. Above all, stay your attack, if one has been started, and concentrate on the problem of co-ordinating your forces.

By making a complete analysis of the position in the manner I have outlined, you will arrive at a perception of any peculiarity attached to it, of its idea. Of the two divisions of the analysis, the first the "mechanical" part, is almost wholly impersonal. It is little more than a matter of arithmetic. The second is qualitative rather than quantitative, and is, of course, by far the more difficult. Great players, who are highly gifted and have had much experience, practically confine themselves to this second part of the complete analysis, feeling it to be superfluous to go through the preliminary mechanical stages, and in general they are justified. Yet it not seldom happens that such players, even the best among them, will differ widely in their opinions on the value of their positions, and may even misjudge them : so that for them, too, it is the part of wisdom to go through, when occasion requires it, the complete analysis in the order indicated. If this is true of great players, the necessity for inexperienced players to make a complete and thorough analysis is obvious. Only by so doing will they have a solid foundation on which to base their judgment, which is only called into play when the first quantitative part of the analysis has been performed. And as this is not subject to opinion, but is purely exterior or mechanical, they start the interior part of the analysis with a solid basis of facts on which to build, and will with greater ease grasp the idea inherent in the position. Janowski, one of the most brilliant of masters, was once asked how he managed to play simultaneous games so well, making his moves, as he

had to do, almost without thinking. He answered :
"I play them as well as I do serious games. I see
at once what move to make in a given position. In
a tournament I would verify this by analysis, in a
simultaneous display I do not, but I know that it is
a good move." This is possible for a very strong
player since he grasps the idea of a position at once,
and therefore knows what course to take. The
inexperienced player, on the other hand, must find
the idea, and to succeed in this his only safe course is
to make the complete analysis, considering one after
the other each piece on the board, both his own and
those of his opponent, estimating their actual and
potential strength, their degree of co-operation, etc.

The interior analysis of a position leads us to
the understanding of its character, but its real idea
can be estimated at its true value only by an individual analysis. This is the third and last part of
the analysis, and has to do especially with the
peculiarities of the position.

Suppose that in one position one has castled
on the K side, and suppose that we have the same
position except that one has castled QR, all remains
equal, space and time, the liaison of the pieces and
their strength. And nevertheless the whole meaning
of the position is changed, and perhaps the game
which was won in the first case will be lost now.
Generally an interior analysis will discover this
peculiarity of the positions, but sometimes we may
not pay enough attention to it, because sometimes
such a peculiarity appears to be of less importance.
An unprotected piece, an undeveloped piece, etc.
Sometimes they have great importance, but sometimes it is only a question of a couple of moves to
put them right. Therefore it is necessary to con-

centrate your mind on such a peculiarity, as therein may lie the whole idea of the position, or the possibility for a tactical combination. That is what we call the individual analysis of a position, the last degree of a complete analysis. It is not only of the highest value in combination in every game, but also in quiet positional play, because very often on such peculiarities we can construct our plan.

Do not play too quickly. Inexperienced players are too often impatient. They want to get to the end quickly, and jib at the time spent in a complete analysis of the position, with the result that they do not fathom its peculiarities, the differences between their game and that of their opponent, the weaknesses, threats, the chances on either side, etc. Failing to do this, they often lose a game which, with a little care, they might otherwise have at least drawn and perhaps won. To see at a glance what is the proper course to take is only given to the very strong player of great experience. The tyro cannot safely neglect the complete triple analysis, quantitative, qualitative, and individual or interior, which we have indicated.

I will now give an example to show how the analysis of a position can guide you to the correct line of play. In the position shown on Diagram 6 (from the game Capablanca—Yates, New York, 1924) the material is equal. White has certainly gained in space, and in time probably. Moreover, his P's are better placed, for Black has two isolated P's, one of them, the P at QR4, very weak, since, standing on a Black square, it cannot be defended by the B, while the Black Kt cannot come to its support without a great loss of time. The problem for White is how best to attack Black's QRP a second time.

DIAGRAM 6

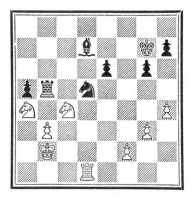

The idea is therefore discovered.   The precise manner in which White wins the pawn is very pretty : 1 Kt—B3, R—B4 ; 2 Kt—K4, R—Kt4 ; 3 Kt(K4)—Q6, R—B4 ; 4 Kt—Kt7, R—B2 ; 5 Kt(Kt7)×P, and wins.

The combination we have just seen is a forced one, for by a series of direct threats against the Black R White was able to gain his objective, the win of the RP, the Kt being pinned because of the unprotected B, which just makes possible this tactical manœuvre. The issue in the position shown on Diagram 7, taken from a tournament game, Teichmann-Bernstein, is not so simple, nevertheless a complete analysis will enable us to elaborate an extended plan of action.   I take it for granted that you can yourself now make the first, mechanical, part of the analysis, so I will pass direct to the second and individual part.

It is not difficult to see the peculiarities of the position. Black has two very weak squares, his KB3 and KR3, "holes" caused by the advance of his KKtP. These are at present defended only by

DIAGRAM 7

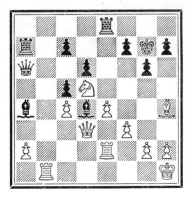

the K, who, however, can eventually be reinforced by his Black B. If, then, this B can be exchanged, these squares will become still weaker, and moreover, White's Q will be able to seize and control one of the long diagonals QR1—KR8 or QB1—KR6, and with the aid of the Kt will be able to establish herself on one of the weak squares, when the danger to the Black King will be extreme. This, then, is the main peculiarity of the position. The question is : Can White force the exchange of this B ? If he can, all is well ; if not, then Black, with his two B's, one of them firmly established at his Q5, will stand better. However, by 1 B—B2, White can force the exchange, and the last act of the drama will run as follows : 1 B—B2, B×B (forced, for if B—K4, 2 P—KB4 and the B has no good square to retreat to) ; 2 R×B, Q—R4 (to prevent Q—B3 ch.) ; 3 Q—K2 (and Black has no adequate defence against Q—Kt2 ch.), P—KB3. White now begins a direct attack on the Black K, in which the hole at KB6 will play the chief role. Thus : 4 Q—Kt2, R—KB1 ; 5 P—Kt4, P—R3 ; 6 P—R4, P—Kt4 (to parry the threat

P—Kt5) ; but there follows : 7 P—KB4, P×R P;
8 Kt×KBP, and wins.

It is not a move,
even the best
move, that you
must seek, but a
realisable plan.
These two examples enable us
to draw the conclusion that our
play must be based on an
analysis of the position, and
that this analysis will indicate
the idea to be followed out, the
objective which we must set
ourselves. It is not a question of finding one more
or less good move. That is the mistake so many
amateurs make. An isolated move has no meaning.
It is only when taken in its context as one of a
sequence of moves that it acquires significance. In
playing we must have a definite idea of the object
which we wish to attain, and then make our moves
with this one idea in view. We do not play merely
from move to move but by series of moves, which
must conform to our plan. Too many players rack
their brains to find in any given position the best,
the winning move, and fail to find it, for they ignore
the relation it must have with what has gone before
or is to follow. If you have a definite plan, it will
not be difficult to find the move best suited to its
furtherance at any particular moment. It is just as
in a discussion. If one has no definite opinion on
the subject at issue, he just chatters on, makes, it
may be, clever remarks, but they will be of little or
no importance, since they lead to no conclusion.
If, however, he has a definite opinion, his remarks
will always be to the point, and he will find the
right words with which to defend it. So in Chess,
at a given moment there may be several good moves
which you could make, but only that one must be
chosen which supports your Chess opinion. Thus

will your game be a logical development of an idea
which has inspired you from the beginning.   True,
you cannot start a game with a complete detailed
plan in your mind, but you can have a general aim,
which will give you your orientation, and with every
move your aim will become more definite.   You will
have developed your pieces with the idea of giving
battle in one part of the board or another, of
attempting to carry the enemy position by assault,
or of wearing out his resistance, and you plan your
series of moves in accordance.

You know, probably, the strange first move
in the Alekhin defence :   1 P—K4, Kt—KB3.
Regarded as an isolated move this looks to be not
only bizarre but weak, for White by advancing his
centre P's can drive the Kt all over the board till
he finally finds sanctuary on the poor square QKt3.
The opening moves in the main variation run thus :
1 P—K4, Kt—KB3 ; 2 P—K5, Kt—Q4 ; 3 P—QB4,
Kt—Kt3 ; 4 P—Q4.   At first sight it would appear
that Black has a very bad game, with only one piece
developed which after three moves finds itself in an
inferior position ; whereas White's centre P's are
developed and seem to control the centre.   There
is, however, a real idea in this defence, which, when
we discover it, will force us to change our first
opinion.   Black's plan is, in fact, to provoke the very
advance of White's P's which we have seen made.
White, moreover, will now have to develop his pieces
behind his pawns, whereas Black plans to develop
his in front of them, and therefore more effectively.
His P's, meanwhile, which have as yet not moved,
will attack White's P centre as occasion offers.
Black has now such an opportunity, and challenges
the centre with 4 ......, P—Q3, to which, if he

wishes to preserve his central pawn formation, White
will reply 5 P—KB4. But then after 5 ......, P × P;
6 BP × P, Black again attacks the centre, at the same
time developing a piece by 6 ......, Kt—QB3.
If now White defends his QP with Kt—KB3, Black
pins the Kt by B—Kt5, thus developing a piece
without loss of time, so he plays instead 7 B—K3 ;
and after 7 ......, B—B4, Black threatens with
Kt—Kt5 and P—QB4 again to attack the centre.

You see, then, that there is really a great idea
underlying the strange move 1 ......, Kt—KB3,
which standing alone would have no interest to us.
It is in the series of moves initiated by it, each one
the logical sequence of the preceding one, and all
subservient to the idea underlying the defence, that
the interest and value of 1 ......, Kt—KB3 lie.   A
good move is always one which carries in its train a
long sequence of other moves, with each one of which,
as it is made, the threat and the danger foreshadowed
in the first one becomes more and more apparent.

The same is true of all openings, and this is
why, as I have said, you must not play your opening
moves automatically, and without thought.   To find
the best moves great Masters, with years of experience, engage in laborious research, and the moves
thus found are blindly repeated by amateurs without
any attempt to fathom their real meaning and how
and why they stand in their context.   You must
give each move real thought, and not only each
move but the series of moves depending on it.
Thus only will you be able logically to develop the
idea which inspired your first move.   This cannot
too often be insisted on.   To make a sequence of
isolated moves, having no bearing on one another,
is like beating the air.

Do not despise the small details; it is often in them that the idea of the position will be found.

In the QP opening, after the moves: 1 P—Q4, P—Q4; 2 P—QB4, P—QB3; 3 P—K3, P—K3; 4 Kt—QB3, Kt—KB3; 5 Kt—KB3, QKt—Q2; 6 B—Q3, B—Q3; 7 O—O, O—O; we arrive at the position shown on Diagram 8.

DIAGRAM 8

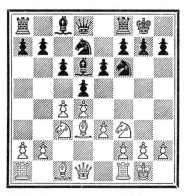

The analysis of this is not difficult. To begin with, the only difference in White's and Black's position is that White's QBP is at its 4th, and his QKt at QB3, while Black's QBP is at its 3rd, and his QKt at Q2. This difference is too small to allow us to base a detailed plan of action on it. Generally the difference is great enough to enable us to see the idea of the position as a whole and to make some definite plan. If, as in this case, it is not, an analysis will still indicate your course to you. You first of all notice that in your QB you have an undeveloped piece. As you cannot make any plan of attack at the moment, your obvious policy will be to get this B into play, for by so doing you will

unite your R's, and thus kill two birds with one
stone. The question, then, is how and where to
develop this piece. There are only two feasible ways
of doing this : (a) to play P—K4 and then develop
your QB at KB4 or KKt5, and (b) to play P—QKt3
and follow this by B—Kt2. You have now to decide
which course is the better, or rather which you
prefer. To make your decision you must be able
to foresee the general course which events will take
in either case. For again, it cannot be repeated too
often, a move to be good must be one of a series of
moves which logically furthers your plan. If it
bears no relation to this, it will be useless, and
having moved a piece, to a square which looks good
and commands perhaps a file or diagonal, you do
not know what to do with it afterwards, as it is out
of the picture of your plan. So in the present
position you must ask what you will do later, when
you have got your QB to QKt2, or to KB4 or KKt5,
as the case may be. We will examine both alternatives :

(a) We propose to develop our QB at KKt5
if possible, so we make the preliminary move 8
P—K4, and, ignoring for the moment what our
opponent may do, how his idea may clash with
ours and force us to modify our plan in detail, we
form in our minds an ideal picture of the situation
after a sequence of moves which we should like to
make, if not prevented by the enemy. And first of
all we notice that after P—K4, P—K5 will drive
away Black's KKt, leaving his KRP undefended
except by the K. Moreover, Black will have to do
something to avoid the loss of a piece, in the
present position, after P—K5 which forks Black's B
and Kt, again that after B—KKt5, the same move
threatens the Kt which is now pinned. We therefore

make in our mind the following ideal sequence of
moves leading to an ultimate attack on Black's K :
8 P—K4, 9 B—KKt5, 10 P—K5, 11 B—B2, 12
Q—Q3, 13 QR—K1, when our development will be
complete, and our attack in full flood. This ideal
picture is shown in Diagram 9. What actually
happened will be shown later under Diagram 15.

DIAGRAM 9

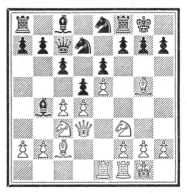

(b) We will now see what happens if we develop
our QB at QKt2. After P—QKt3 and B—Kt2,
the B has a very limited range of action, for the
long diagonal, on which it is, is blocked by a White
P at Q4. We must therefore seek to extend the
effect of the B in this diagonal, and this we can
clearly do by posting our KKt at K5 (after clearing
the line in the immediate neighbourhood of the B
by QKt—K2), for now the B helps to support the
strongly posted Kt at K5. This Kt can be further
supported by P—KB4, after which with the moves
Kt—KKt3, Q—KB3, say, and QR—K1 we shall
again have completed our development, but the
resulting ideal configuration of our pieces, see
Diagram 10, differs greatly from that in Diagram 9,

and leads to an entirely different kind of attack.
Let us remark, in passing, that to see a player
confuse these totally different plans, inconsequently
making moves, some corresponding to the first,
others to the second, is a truly piteous spectacle !

DIAGRAM 10

Do not think too soon about what your opponent can do; first get clear what you want to do.

You will have noticed that so far we have given no consideration to what our opponent can do. And this is right, for we must first get clear in our mind what our general plan is to be. If you have the initiative, and remember that White always starts with this advantage, you must strive to keep it. You must construct your plan, which, do not forget, will be based on the actual position facing you without giving too much thought to what your opponent can do whether in defence or offence. You must determine to make him dance to your tune. If you are forever thinking of what he may possibly threaten, you will soon lose the will to conquer, the initiative will pass out of your hands, and it will be your opponent who then will call the tune, and you will be lucky if you save the game. On the other hand, if your opponent has the initiative, as he will at the start if you are Black, you must obviously give careful thought to his moves, so that you may meet his immediate threats, and fathom the plan which he is forming, while all the time you will keep your eyes very open for the chance by a timely thrust to seize the initiative from him.

To return to the position given on Diagram 8. What was said for White is equally true for Black, since the positions are practically identical. Black also can develop his QB in two ways, at QKt2 or KKt5. He must play for one or the other, since the development of his QB is the main problem he has to solve. There is, however, this difference between Black's and White's positions : that Black's QB, if developed at QKt2, will have the long diagonal obstructed by two of his own P's, at QB3 and Q4, so that if placed there his effect may for some considerable time be greatly restricted. It will therefore be better for him to prepare for its development at Kt5 by P—K4.

Do not lose confidence in your judgment. There is an important remark which must be made here. White, shall we say, has decided that it is better to develop his QB at KKt5 than at QKt2, and with this in view plays P—K4. Suppose now that Black plays P—QKt3 and B—Kt2, getting his B, that is to say, on the long diagonal. On this many players in White's position suddenly get anxious and lose confidence : visions of a mating attack in the long diagonal begin to haunt them ; they wonder if they did wrong in developing the QB as they did. This is all very foolish. The positions are so nearly identical that what is good for White must also be good for Black. White has decided that the development of his QB by P—K4 is the better plan, the one giving greater chances. Let him have the courage of his convictions, and not lose heart, if he sees his opponent choose a course which he has deliberately rejected. Optimism is a great moral asset in Chess, but confidence in oneself is literally essential if we want to play the game at all. A defeatist spirit must lead to disaster.

We will now suppose that White and Black have both decided to develop their QB's by playing P—K4 (see Diagram 8). It is White's move and he plays 8 P—K4. Black at once sees that White threatens to win a piece by P—K5, so before executing his own plan he must find a defence to this threat. What is he to do ? The obvious 8 ......, P × KP solves his immediate problem, and if this were all he had to think about, he would certainly make the move. But he has also to consider the bearing of 8 ......, P × KP on his real problem, the development of his QB. How will this be affected ? After, e.g., 8 ......, P × KP ; 9 Kt × P, Kt × Kt ; 10 B × Kt, P—K4 ; 11 P × P, Kt × P ; 12 Kt × Kt, B × Kt ; 13 B × RP ch., K × B ; 14 Q—R5ch., followed by Q × B, White has won a P. If, therefore, Black captures the KP, he will be unable himself to play P—K4, and the problem of developing his QB will remain unsolved. He must therefore find another defence against the threat. If no other is to be found, we must then assume that he has made some mistake previously. However, before submitting to such an assumption, Black must carefully examine the position, always with the one thought in his mind, that whatever defence to White's immediate threat be chosen, it must not prejudice his real plan, namely, to play P—K4. He can, of course, retire the Kt or B, but in either case this would mean the loss of a move, and therefore of a valuable tempo, besides allowing White to play P—K5, for ever stopping him from playing P—K4. Black must therefore somehow or other gain a move, and this he can do by 8 ......, P×BP ! White must reply 9 B×BP, which brings his B on to a less favourable diagonal, and Black gains the time necessary to play 9 ......, P—K4, when his main difficulty in this opening will have to be overcome.

Never lose sight of your general idea, however thick the fight.   There is a moral in all this, which must be laid to heart. However hard pressed you may be, never forget the general plan of action which you had formed. If, in the example we have been considering, Black had lost his head, had not kept his main idea (development of his QB by means of P—K4) constantly in view, he would have fared badly. And this is what so many amateurs actually do. Faced by a serious enemy threat, they content themselves with finding a move which will parry the immediate danger, without considering whether that move will serve their plan, or actually make it impossible of execution. They forget in the stress of the fight that they too had a plan, and perhaps a thoroughly good and sound one, and throw away all their chances of carrying it out. When the immediate danger is past they will likely again remember their plan, and try to further it, but it will then generally be too late. They may have temporarily repulsed the attack, they will be lost nevertheless, for their game will have been compromised by their inattention to their main interest.

You will have noticed the important part played by the QB in the position we have been discussing. Once you have discovered that the peculiarity of the position lies in this B, and have decided that the best way to develop it is by P—K4, you must go to any lengths, attempt the impossible even, to carry through your design.

Do not modify your plan. Order. Counter-order. Disorder ! In Chess, as in war, these are the worst sort of tactics. Therefore, hold to your main idea, however difficult the position may seem. If you are forced to abandon it, you will have to bow to the inevitable, for necessity knows no law. But you must not too readily submit to the conclusion that you are so forced. This would mean that you considered that your opponent had already outplayed you. If, however, a careful analysis of the position convinces that you stand as well as he does, do not tamely submit to his will. A way must be sought, as in the example under discussion, to meet the enemy threat and at the same time further your main plan. Of course, if you have no definite plan you are beaten before you begin to play. If you have, do not too readily admit to an inferiority complex.

Our last example was taken from the opening. We will now take one from the middle game, rather more complicated than the ones considered under Diagrams 5 and 6, which were very simple since the combinations illustrated were almost forced.

In the position shown in Diagram 11 (from a game Nimzowitsch—Capablanca) Black has the advantage in time and space, since he has gained

two moves, and controls the centre. The forces on
each side are equal and no weaknesses are visible in
the configuration of the pawns. Black's superiority
is clear in that all his pieces are, or can quickly be,
in play, including his QB, while White's QB is not
only undeveloped, but it will take time to develop it,
since this cannot be effected by P—K4, without

DIAGRAM 11

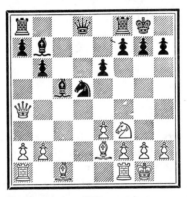

seriously weakening the KP, and meanwhile White's
R's will remain unconnected, so that virtually Black
has three pieces more in play than White, whose only
method of developing his QB is by P—QKt3 and
B—Kt2. White, therefore, must plan to bring his
QB into play and unite his R's, while Black will of
course put every obstacle in his way, and utilise
every tempo gained to bring his pieces into commanding positions, for if he passively allowed White
to carry out his plan unmolested his present
superiority would evaporate.

Such is the game of Chess! A broad plan,
based on a precise analysis of the position, which
will at the same time indicate the method to be
followed in carrying it out. It is not in the heat

of the battle, when perhaps you are menaced on every side, that this broad plan can be quickly thought out. This must be done before embarking on complications, at crucial stages of the struggle. For instance, when passing from the opening to the middle game, or, particularly, from the middle to the end game. We say "particularly," because so many amateurs forget the supreme importance of forming in advance a sound plan based on the position for the concluding stage of the game. In passing out of the opening into the middle game, the pieces are most of them still on the board; complications of all kinds are possible, and the player is forced, by obvious threats or what not, to consider the position with a little care. After the rough and tumble of the middle game, however, when the excitement is over, when little remains on the board except K's and P's, then is the time to take firm hold of oneself, and make a thorough analysis of the now simplified position, with a view to forming a sound plan for the end game. An ill-considered move is less inevitably fatal in the middle game than in the ending. Yet how often we see after general exchanges one side or the other making the first best move which comes into his head, without devising any plan of which this move is to form the first of a series, with the result that in an otherwise even position, his more careful opponent, who has by analysis formed a clear idea of the course to be pursued, will outplay him and win a game which should logically have been drawn. We shall return to this later.

To go back to our Diagram. It is Black's move and he plays :

1. ...... Q—B3

Clearly with the idea of stopping the immediate P—QKt3.

2.	B—R6	B × B
3.	Q × B	Kt—Kt5
4.	Q—K2	KR—Q1

Black, we see, has gained a tempo for the development of one of his R's, while White's plan is not advanced one jot.

5.	P—QR3	Kt—Q6
6.	Kt—K1	Kt × Kt

Here we see one of Capablanca's principles in action : to simplify the game by exchanging pieces (here the Kt) which do not contribute to the superiority of his position, which here resides in the B and two active R's. Incidentally, he has gained another tempo for the development of his QR.

7.	R × Kt	QR—B1
8.	R—QKt1	Q—K4 !

Threatening B—Q3, which will oblige White to create a weakness on the K side by P—KKt3.

Do not be content with attacking an existing weakness; always seek to create others.

In this lies the excellence of Black's last move. His main threat, based on the position of his R's and White's undeveloped state, lies in the invasion of White's 2nd rank by these R's. This invasion will be all the more deadly if White can be made to weaken his K side, which is what Black threatens to do with his last move. Therefore remember : In carrying out your main plan, which will be directed against some enemy weakness, never, in working out the details, neglect the opportunity to create other weaknesses, if such occurs, as it usually will. In the case in point without such a weakening of White's position, his game, though difficult, would be tenable, for there are at present no compromising weaknesses to point to in his position.

9. P—KKt3   Q—Q4

It is now a fitting time to take a census of the position afresh. In time the two sides are equal : each has made the same number of effective moves. They differ, however, greatly in value, for Black has a firmer hold on the centre than ever, his R's commanding open files, are far better placed, and White's K side is compromised by P—KKt3. Black can no longer prevent the development of White's QB. Indeed, after P—QKt4, Black's KB will be forced to give up his commanding position. The White R's are still ill placed. It will take time for him to get them into better positions, which time can be occupied by Black in the invasion by his R's of White's position, the effect of which will be all the more deadly, as already pointed out, through the weakness of White's K side P's.

10. P—QKt4   B—B1

A very important move. It is often difficult to determine on the best square to which to retire a piece, which has been forced away from a commanding position. By retiring to B1, he (1) shields his K from possible checks when his R's have invaded the enemy base, (2) protects his KKtP in case of mating attacks in the long diagonal. The alternative was B—K2 (clearly B—Q3, obstructing the R would have been idle, now that White has already been forced to weaken his K side by P—KKt3), but there is no obvious use to be made of the diagonal Q1—KR5, and the definite ends attained by B—B1 would not be realised.

11. B—Kt2   Q—R7

With the desperate threat of P—QR4, which
would result in the loss to White of his QRP.

12.   R—R1   . . . . . .

White's difficulties are mounting. He has now
to try to meet the imminent invasion of his 2nd
rank by the enemy R's.

12. . . . . . .   Q—Kt6
13.   B—Q4   . . . . .

Hoping to shut out at least one R !

13.   . . . . . .   R—B7
14.   Q—R6   . . . . . .

White seeks counter chances. It might have
been better to retire the Q to the 1st rank, but Black
then with P—KB3 and P—K4 would provide White
with a very difficult problem to solve.

14.   . . . . . .   P—K4 !

A beautiful P sacrifice, which forces open the
road for Black's second R to invade White's 2nd rank.

15.   B×P   R(Q1)—Q7

Now the importance of Black's 8th move,
forcing P—KKt3, is manifest. All the white squares
on the K wing are now weak. The B cannot come
to his K's aid as the only available square (KKt3) is
occupied. You may say Capablanca could not have
foreseen all this. True, he could not analyse all the
possible variations, but he had based his general idea
of attack on an analysis of the position ; he knew
that this attack must be carried out by his R's from
their position on their 7th rank ; it was therefore
clear that he must so devise it that White's QB should
be prevented from getting to KKt3, to protect the
K wing, and since this could be done by simultaneously weakening that wing, his course was clear.
Thus it is that even in the severe fighting in the
middle game, the master, by keeping ever before his

mind his main idea, steers his way through the numberless variations possible in the position.

16.   Q—Kt7   ......

To restore communication with his beleaguered K he must lose a P, for if R—KB1, 16 ......, Q×KP ! and if Q—B1, 16 ......, Q—Q4 ; 17 B—Q4, Q—KR4 ; 18 P—KR4, Q—B6 and wins.

16.	......	R×BP
17.	P—KKt4	Q—K3
18.	B—Kt3	R×KRP !

Another very fine idea.   If B×R, 19 Q×KtP ch. and mate cannot be avoided.   It will have been noticed how with his 17th move White had to create another weakness, in order to allow his KB to come to his K's aid.   One weakness almost invariably brings another in its train.

19.	Q—B3	R(R7)—Kt7 ch.
20.	Q×R	R×Q ch.
21.	K×R	Q×KtP

And Black won easily, having 2 P's more and a Q commanding the board for White's two R's. In this game superiority in time and space has been converted into superiority in force.

This fine game is a striking example of our thesis, that we must play with a definite plan in mind, and that this plan must be based on a careful analysis of the position.   On neither side have there been isolated moves, having no bearing on the general idea ; we have seen only series of moves, logically conceived, through which the position was ever changing, leading therefore to new possibilities. The plan formed by each party was correct, and held to.   If Black won, it was because his initial superiority in position gave him a commanding advantage, assuming that he knew how to exploit it.

If he had given away to his opponent a single tempo, it would have enabled the latter to carry through his plan in time to equalise the game. And all that is required of a player is that he think logically, granted not an easy thing to do, but one for which no special gifts are necessary. It is pure laziness of mind which leads to the distressing sight, so often seen, of moves made without rhyme or reason, having no bearing on the position, let alone any relation to a settled plan.

It must not be thought, however, that in any given game one idea dominates to the extent that the whole game from the first move to the last is a simple development of that idea. Chess, we must remember, is a battle of ideas, and throughout our ideas encounter at every moment those of our opponent. We shall, therefore, in the event, often have to content ourselves with small results, and be glad if in the struggle we can gain some definite positional or other advantage instead of the potentially commanding advantage, for which a complete realisation of our aim might have led us to hope. And even if we have realised our idea, it does not necessarily follow that the game is won. Time alone can prove whether our idea was really a sound one, whether our opponent's idea was not after all a better one. But assuming our idea realised, we have then reached a new position at which a fresh stage of the game may be said to begin, when we shall have to find a new idea, which of course will be in logical sequence to our first, on which to base our future action. It is at this moment essential to take fresh stock of the position, to make a thorough analysis, and never is this truer than at the critical moment when we pass from the middle to the end game.

Do not get care- The example which follows
less when, after shows how chess is played from
general exchanges, one position to another, how in
the end game is each one the ideas inherent in
reached. them must be discovered. When
the new position for which we
have played is reached, then is
the time by a careful analysis to ascertain the idea
underlying it, or to confirm our judgment previously
formed of it when making our plans.

DIAGRAM 12

In the position shown on Diagram 12, it was
Black's move. Analysing the position, we see that
if White has apparently gained one move in time,
Black has the advantage in space, his pieces moreover have greater effective strength, while White's
Q side is entirely undeveloped. Further, Black with
P—Q5 can at once give himself a protected passed P.
However, he sees a better plan, namely, to reduce
the position to an end game, and since White's
moves are almost forced, the following sequence of
moves indicates the plan which Black formed.
1 ......, P×KP; 2 B×P, Kt×B; 3 Q × Kt

Q—Q5 ! 4 Q × Q (if Q × BP, B × P ; and White's QBP will fall in a move or two, while Black still has a passed P) P × Q ; 5 Kt—Q2, B—R3 ; 6 P—QKt3, KR—K1 ; 7 Kt—B3, B—B3 ; 8 B—Kt2, R—K5 ; 9 QR—K1, QR—K1 ; 10 R × R, R × R ; 11 R—K1 (R—Q1 might have offered better resistance) R × R ; 12 Kt × R and we have the position shown on Diagram 13. A clear and easy win for Black, as he had foreseen when he began his combination to force

DIAGRAM 13

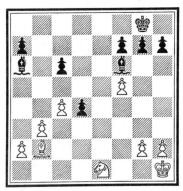

exchanges. He has a passed P, which, after P—QB4, will be a protected passed P. He has his two beautiful B's, one of whom can immediately be brought on to a better diagonal with gain of a tempo, by attacking White's KBP which is in the air. His K, too, is nearer the centre. His obvious plan is to bring his QB round so as to be in a position to support this advance of his passed P. This he can do, as already said, with gain in time, by B—B1. White must defend his KBP and his only way is by P—KKt4, when with P—KR4, Black will threaten to break up White's K side P's, leaving free range of action to his B's. If at any moment White plays

Kt—B3, then P—QB4 protects the P.   Meanwhile
White is condemned to a purely passive role.   He
can only try to blockade Black's QP, and pray for a
chance of getting rid of one of Black's terrible B's,
preferably by exchanging his Kt for the KB, leaving
B's of opposite colour on the board.   Black, however,
instead of taking time to analyse the now clarified
position, hastily played 12 ......, P—QB4 ? and
after 13 Kt—Q3 !, B—K2 ; 14 B—R3, B—QB1
(he has nothing better) ; 15 B×P, B×B ; 16 Kt×B,
B×P, saw his whole advantage vanish.

*Haste, the great
enemy.*

Haste is never more dangerous
than when you feel that victory
is in your grasp.   It is at this
critical moment that there is a
terrible tendency to forget ordinary caution, to
become careless, to relax in accuracy, or on the
other hand to be over-timid, giving the alert enemy
his chance to extricate himself.   Never is cold
reason, clear thinking, more necessary than when
victory is in sight.   And as we have already insisted
more than once : it is when passing from one stage
of the game to the next, that the greatest care should
be taken, and a census of the position at these
critical moments should never be omitted.   For it
is through thoughtless haste at such moments that
countless games are only drawn, or more often lost,
which might have been won with great ease, but for
careless over-confidence.

*Do not relax in
the hour of victory.*

When you have a clear won
position, then is the time when
you must be most careful not
to relax your attention, and, by
a careless or inconsequent move, give your opponent
drawing or winning chances.   The number of games

thus thrown away is legion, and the example given
in Diagram 14 shows that even the mightiest master
sometimes falls into this error. It occurred in a
game between Alekhin (White) and Yates in the
Hastings Tournament of 1922.

It is White's move, and Black's position is
desperate. His one conceivable hope lies in Q—
K6 ch., for then if the K moves to R2 (if K—R1,

DIAGRAM 14

mate in two follows by Q—R6 ch., and Q×P mate)
Black with Q×KP ch. and Q—Kt2 wins a P and is
safe ; in fact will have a won game. White will
therefore have to interpose the R, which will then be
pinned. White could and should have ignored this
threatened pin, and played at once B—Kt6 when
Black to avoid mate would have at best to give up his
Q for a R and B. For instance : 1 B—Kt6, Q—
K6 ch. ; 2 R—B2, K—K1 ; 3 B×P ch., K—Q2 !
4 R×B ch., P×R ; 5 B×P dis. ch., K—K1 ; 6 Q—
Kt8 ch., K—K2 ; 7 Q—B7 ch., K—Q1 ; 8 Q—B8 ch.,
K—Q2 ; 9 P—K6 ch., and wins. White, however,
thought he might as well safeguard himself against
the pin of his R, so sacrificed the exchange by

1 R×B, P×R ; 2 B—Kt6, K—K1. No real harm
has so far been done, for he has still a clear win by
3 Q—Kt8 ch., K—Q2 ; 4 Q×P ch., K—B3 ; 5 Q—
K6 ch., K—Kt2 ; 6 Q×QP ch., K—Kt1 ; 7 B—K4,
R—B3 ; 8 P—Kt4, P—R3 ; 9 P—R4 and wins. But
instead of this, White played 3 R×P ? ? Black
seized his chance with both hands, as might be
expected of so enterprising a master, and never gave
his formidable adversary a chance. The game proceeded : 3 . . . . . ., R—B8 ch. ; 4 K—B2 (Desperation.
If R—B1 dis. ch., Black's K gets to safety at his
QKt1, since his R at B8 is guarded by the Q) Q—
R5 ch. ; 5 K—K3, Q—K8 ch. ; 6 K—B3, R(B1)—
B6 ch. ! ; 7 P×R, R×P ch. ; 8 B—Q3, Q—B8 ch. ;
9 K—K3, R×B ch. ; 10 Q×R, Q×Q ch. ; 11 K×Q,
K×R and wins easily.

In the Nimzowitsch-Capablanca game we saw
how Black converted the advantage he had in a
well-developed B into one based on the position of
his R's. He had therefore two concurrent ideas : to
delay the development of White's B as long as
possible, and to use the time so gained to bring his
R's into commanding positions. White, on the other
hand, could have but one idea : to develop as speedily
as possible his QB, since until this was effected he
was at serious disadvantage. Black's problem was
therefore the easier. In our next example we shall
meet with a real clash of ideas, in which both opponents form plans based on different, but essentially
sound conceptions.

The position shown on Diagram 15 has arisen
out of that discussed under Diagram 8, when it will
be remembered we saw in Diagram 9 the vision
which was before White's eyes when he determined
on a plan for developing his QB at KKt5. Diagram 8

DIAGRAM 15

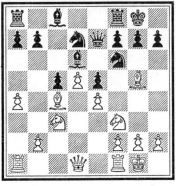

was an ideal picture of the vision, which took into no
account the ideas which Black might form, or the
inevitable changes in detail which would be forced
on White by this conflict of ideas. Now in Diagram
15 we have the actual picture which was evolved out
of this conflict, and a mere comparison of the two
situations is in itself instructive.

Let us, as always, begin by an analysis of the
position. It is Black's move (the intervening moves
were 8 P—K4, P×BP; 9 B×P, P—K4; 10 B—
KKt5, Q—K2; 11 P—Q5, P—QB4; 12 P—QR4);
therefore White is one and not two moves to the
good. The positions are almost equal. White has
a protected passed pawn at Q5, but to balance this
Black has a majority of P's on the Q side. It was to
counteract any disagreeable effect their advance might
have in the middle game, that White played P—QR4.
At the moment they can do little ; in the end game,
however, they may constitute a real danger, especially
in view of White's backward QKtP (a pawn is said
to be "backward" when it cannot advance without
coming under the fire of an enemy P on an adjacent
file, and is itself unsupported by a P in such an

advance).   White, in view of his beautiful protected passed P at Q5, is stronger in the centre.   Against a passive defence, White would with every move strengthen his position until his superiority became overwhelming.   What then shall Black undertake ? He has really little choice.   Since he can do nothing for the moment on the Q side, he must attempt an attack on the K side.

The problem is how to carry out such an attack, for White has no present weakness on his K side. He can gain a move by attacking White's QB.   To maintain the pin White will probably retire his B to KR4, and at once Black recognises his KB5 as a potentially strong square for him, betraying therefore the only weakness, if so it can be called, in White's K side position.   If Black can establish a Kt there, it will be very strongly placed, directly attacking as it would, the White K's stronghold.   If White, chafing under the restraint, and wishing to be rid of the threats hanging over him, drive the Kt away by P—KKt3 the Kt will have amply fulfilled his mission, for White's K side P's will be seriously weakened, there will be disagreeable "holes" at his KB3 and KR3, and in fact his whole position on this side of the board will be compromised.   The only question is how to get the Kt to this square; always remembering that Black's original plan, the development of his QB, must never be lost sight of.   This at once suggests the proper plan.   It is his QKt whom Black must detail for this important service, with orders to travel via KB1 and KKt3, and you will notice that with his first move Kt—KB1, the Kt clears the road for the QB.   However, before starting the Kt in his raid, Black must prepare a sufficient defence for his Kt when he shall reach KB5.   This

he must do by P—KKt4, again with gain of time.
If he failed to make this provision, White could
exchange this Kt when it reached KB5, and, since
Black would have to recapture with his KP, White's
centre P's would be strengthened.

Let us, then, assume that Black has been able
to carry out his plan unopposed. The sequence of
moves : P—KR3, P—KKt4, R—K1, Kt—B1, Kt—
Kt3, Kt—B5 will bring about the configuration of
Black's pieces shown in Diagram 12. This again
gives us an ideal picture of what could happen, if
there were no conflict of ideas to modify the picture.

DIAGRAM 16

And this leads to a very important point. It is this
ideal picture which you must build up in your mind
when forming a plan, based of course on your
analysis of the position. It is worse than idle to
attempt to anticipate every possible reply your
opponent may make to each of
your proposed moves. You will
but waste your time ; in fact
you will only lose yourself in a
maze of calculations which can
have no end. Never, therefore,

*Do not entangle
yourself in a
maze of calcula-
tions.*

do what so many less experienced players do in analysing a position, eternally putting the question to themselves : "If I do this, he will do that—or that —or that," ad infinitum ! First form your ideal picture on the supposition that your opponent does nothing. With this picture clear in your mind, then is the time to ask your self what general plan your opponent may form to counter yours ; whether he may have some definite plan inherent in the position, which you in turn will have to counter, while keeping your own in view ; whether finally your idea is really capable of execution, and whether it really carries the threat your ideal picture promises. Exact calculations are in general only possible in combinations in which your opponent's moves are largely forced, as for instance in the example given under Diagram 6.

Let us now return to Diagram 15. To carry out his plan Black plays :

12. ...... P—KR3

White cannot be sure whether this move is the beginning of an attack or has merely the object of releasing his Kt from the pin ; so he has only at the moment to decide to which square to retire his B, and he will certainly keep up the pin with :

13. B—R4 R—K1

Black's move is readily intelligible to White. Black clearly wants to develop his QB—this had been the object of his P—K4, he must therefore free a square for his Kt, which is obstructing the B. With R—K1 he not only provides an admirable square for his Kt, whence it protects his KR2 and watches the squares K3 and KKt3, but also brings his R into play in a file where he may well be needed either for the protection of his KP or to hold White's

KP. So much is obvious. White, however, must
not be content with this. Has Black not some
ulterior object in this move Kt—B1 ? What is
probably his whole plan ?   If White does not fathom
Black's idea in time, he will likely find himself too
late to organise an adequate defence to it. His
analysis of the position will have shown him that
Black at the moment can undertake nothing useful
on the Q side, and his move Kt—B1 is a clear
indication that he is preparing a K side attack, and
is aiming to plant his QKt at his KB5. And rapidly
he in his turn forms the ideal picture which Black
has in his mind (Diagram 16). White then reflects :
Is this position so dangerous to him that Black must
be prevented from realising it at any cost ? If it is
not so dangerous as all this, what defence must be
organised against it ? Will Black create any weakness
in his own position while carrying it out ?

Again, emphasis must be laid on the proper
method of dealing with the problems which arise
during a game of Chess. White here quite properly
does not attempt to consider every Black move, but
tries to foresee and understand his whole general
plan ; and to find a general defence against it. If we
only think of finding a defence against each isolated
move, without considering that move as one in a
series made in relation to a general plan, our defence
must eventually break down, since our moves will
be out of relation to it. In the case under consideration it is not so very difficult to form a counter
plan to Black's threat. Suppose Black's QKt is
aiming for his KB5 ; well, White's Kt can also make
a similar raid and arrive at his KB5. White's Kt at
KB5 will then threaten Black's K position precisely
as Black's Kt would threaten White, only the threats

will be more acute, for Black's K's position will already have been compromised by the advance of his KR and KKt P's, and, more important, if White can plant his Kt at KB5, it can never be driven away by a P. So White plays :

14. Kt—Q2   . . . . . .

Without the previous discussion, you might not, in playing over the game, have understood the object of this move, which withdraws the KKt from a beautiful square to one where it apparently has no future. You now know that he is starting on his journey to his KB5. This, however, is only a part of the picture which White has formed. He has penetrated Black's plan, realises that in its execution his QB will be driven to KKt3, where it will be in a veritable desert as far as its future is concerned, so that his whole plan involves not only the Kt's journey to KB5 via B4, K3 or B1 and Kt3, but also B—QKt3 or R2, Kt—B4—K3—B5 (or R—K1, Kt—B1—Kt3 —B5), but also P—KB3 and B—KB2, where the B will be on a splendid diagonal with an attack on Black's QBP. This game is interesting in that we have the inevitable conflict of ideas, but here one side, Black, has not really penetrated the whole of his opponent's plan, whereas his is an open book to White. Seeing, therefore, in Kt—Q2 merely a defensive move to his threat, made to allow P—KB3 and the withdrawal of White's QB to B2, and nothing else, he at once, with the idea of gaining a tempo, plays :

14. . . . . . .   P—KKt4
15. B—KKt3   Kt—KB1
16. P—KB3   Kt—Kt3
17. B—B2   . . . . .

Please pay the greatest attention to this move.

Its value lies in the attack on Black's QBP, which Black will eventually have to spend time in defending, and in the release of the square KKt3, allowing P—KKt3 should Black venture now to plant his Kt at his KB5.

But it has a more general meaning. The B at KKt3 had no open line before him, as a matter of fact he was weaker than a P because a P could stop Black's Kt coming to KB4, which the B cannot do. He even stops his own KKtP driving the Kt away, should it actually come to KB4. At KB2 on the contrary, the B becomes powerful as he forces his opponent to think about the defence of his QBP, instead of going straightaway to his attack on the K side. Many times during the game we shall notice the strength of this B here and how uncomfortable he is to the enemy.

17.   ......   K—Kt2 ?

This move proves that Black has not understood White's plan, else he would not have placed his K where it will be exposed to a check from his KB4, when White's Kt occupies that square. If Black lost this game it was not on account of any directly bad play on his part, but because he did not fathom the enemy plan, until it was too late to find an adequate defence to it. Another proof, if more be needed, of the necessity for a thorough analysis of the position, both from your own and from your opponent's point of view, for making a sound plan of your own, and for anticipating your opponent's plan, as suggested by that analysis. Black has been misled by White's play. So far the latter's moves have appeared to be purely defensive, and Black did not detect any preparation for an attack. There is, however, a serious menace.

What must White's whole plan really be ? It is not difficult to see. His real superiority lies in his protected passed P at Q5. Black must never if he can help it allow this P to advance. And here, in order fully to understand the situation, a short digression is necessary. If your opponent should have a passed pawn, your first and most urgent duty is *Never omit to* mechanically to stop its ad- *blockade an enemy* vance—blockade it. This you *passed pawn.* must do by placing a piece, the less valuable the better, on the square fronting it. Such a piece Nimzowitsch calls "der blockeur," or the blockader. Now as long as the blockader remains at his post the passed pawn is mechanically pre- vented from advancing. The efforts of the lucky owner of such a pawn will obviously be directed towards raising the blockade, either by exchanging or by driving off the blockader, when his passed pawn will be free to pursue its journey.

Black should have taken all this into his calcula- tions when analysing the position and asked himself in time, what measures will White be able to take to clear the road for the advance of his QP. Black's Q3 is at present the critical square, the one which he must keep occupied in order to blockade the passed pawn. White's moves so far have therefore only been tactical elements in his strategical plan, which must, if he analysed the position correctly, as he did, be directed against his Q6, as the first part of his campaign to advance his QP. He now discloses his hand with

18. Kt—Kt5   . . . . . .

Black must seek to maintain the blockade, so he occupies his second line of defence with

18.	......	B—Q2
19.	Kt × B	Q × Kt
20.	B—Kt5	......

Always with the same idea, namely, to demolish the blockade. White had to be a little careful here and examine the effect of 20 ......, B × B ; 21 P × B. Of course, if 21 ......, Q—Kt3 ; 22 Kt—B4, Q × P ; 23 Kt—Q6 wins the exchange. The possible danger which he had to estimate lay in the resulting isolated doubled P's on the QKt file. The compensation he would have in the two open files, QR and QB, for his R's would, however, more than balance the weakness of these P's. He need not even have faced this risk, if so it can be called, for he could, with precisely the same end in view, have taken a longer road by Q—Kt3 (or K2), B—Kt5, and lastly Kt—B4.

| 20. | ...... | P—QKt3 |

Do not leave your pieces in bad positions.

Black recognises all this and therefore does not take the B, but hastens, while there is yet time, to defend his precious P at QB4, which would be unprotected after 21 B × B, Q × B. Truly White's QB in his new position at KB2 has become a powerful attacking force. What an ignominious role he would have had to play, if he had remained at KKt3 ! barely more than that of a pawn masquerading in a mitre. An excellent example this to illustrate the maxim : If you have a piece badly placed, or whose range of action is restricted, make it your first business to provide him with a better position. In this game White's forethought in doing this for his QB made possible, at any rate rendered far easier, the accomplishment of his purpose.

| 21. | Kt—B4 | ...... |

White does not at once take the B, since by the text move he can gain a tempo by attacking the Q.

21.	......	Q—K2
22.	B × B	Q × B
23.	P—R5 !	......

White could here have played at once Kt—K3, threatening Kt—B5 ch., but he rightly preferred first to induce a weakness on Black's Q·side (cf. the similar tactics employed in the game discussed under Diagram 11), and thus to increase the effective strength of his QB. There was, however, another consideration of great importance involved.

We can gain nothing in Chess except by means of threats. Now threats may be of various kinds : direct or indirect, real or merely apparent, etc. They may also be immediate or remote, and it is here that the greatest difference in threats lies. Against an immediate direct threat, it is not in general difficult to find a parry to it, given that the forces on each side are equal. Against a remote threat, you will only succeed in finding a good defence if you foresee it coming many moves ahead, as many moves in fact as your opponent planned it. The case is much more difficult when two threats appear on the board at one time. This can often be brought about by approaching the remote threat by a series of moves each carrying an immediate threat. At a given moment the time will come when the remote threat becomes imminent, and with it another direct immediate threat in our series is also in being. Our opponent in defending himself against the single immediate threats which our moves revealed, had his hands full defending himself against the immediate dangers which faced him at every move, and was unable to make adequate provision against the remote threat, even if he fully realised its approach. And suddenly this remote threat becomes an immediate one and appears coupled with another definite, if subsidiary threat, and his difficulty is great, for he has to choose which one to parry ; he has to determine which of the two evils is the lesser, and submit to this. So here, after

23. ......   P—QKt4
24. Kt—K3   ......

Black suddenly observes that White threatens with his next move Kt—B5 ch., leaving his QBP at the mercy of White's QB. Clearly he cannot afford to lose a pawn, so

24. ......   Q—B2
25. Kt—B5 ch.   K—R2

And White has at last reached the position at which he aimed (see Diagram 17). If his idea was well founded, his judgment correct, then he ought

DIAGRAM 17

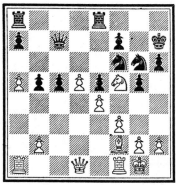

now to have a won game, for he has a passed pawn, unobstructed by any blockade, his Kt is firmly established at KB5, and cannot be driven away, since Black's KKtP has advanced to his 4th, whereas

Black has not yet succeeded in carrying out his plan
of playing his Kt to his KB5, and if he did, P—KKt3
would at once drive him away, if White felt his
presence there irksome. Note, too, the important
role played by White's KKt. When White on his
14th move played Kt—Q2, he certainly could not
have foreseen all the details of the succeeding play ;
but he could and did see that this Kt could reach his
objective, the square KB5, by either of two routes,
via KB1 and KKt3, or via QB4 and K3. He chose
the latter route because in taking it the Kt could
always threaten something, at the same time supporting the attack on Black's Q flank, because, too,
since it was open to him, his Kt would at all stages
be centrally, and therefore better, placed, than if he
had taken the road via KB1 and KKt3, where he
would be completely out of touch for a time with the
central battlefields, and barred from co-operation in
any action on the other flank, and would moreover
advertise the fact that his mission lay on KB5.
By taking what we might call the central route,
Black is left in doubt where eventually White means
to employ this Kt, who from his central position can
quickly come into action, on either wing. Black,
therefore, being in doubt, got into trouble, for he
could not be sure of his own line of play. The
moral is obvious : choose always that continuation
which will allow your pieces the greater freedom of
action, so that your opponent may be left in the dark as
to your real intentions up to the last possible moment.

White has now an ideal offensive position, for
he can launch a double attack on the enemy, one on
his K's position which has been compromised and
weakened by the advance of his KR and KKt P's ;
the other by an advance of his QP which is now

unobstructed. The passed pawn will be still stronger when the board is cleared of pieces, so White will wisely direct his first attack against the enemy King, leaving the advance of the QP, the fear of which will ever haunt Black, till an opportune moment arrives. You will notice that it is the Black squares, KB3, KKt2, and KR3, which have been weakened by the pawn advance. The attack will be directed against them. The method of operation is clearly indicated. The White Kt has already Black's KKt2 and KR3 under attack ; P—KR4 will force a further weakening, and the White Q will take up a position on the diagonal QB1—KR6. It remains to determine where in this diagonal to place the Q. At first sight QB1 looks to be a good square, for from here she will attack Black's QBP, KRP and KKtP simultaneously (after P—KR4, P × P). Black would, however, have an adequate reply in Kt—B5 ! threatening Kt—K7 ch., and the win of the Q. So this pretty plan must be renounced and the Q posted at Q2. In Chess, as in life, you seldom get all you want, and have to content yourself with what you can get, provided it brings you nearer your goal.

If we analyse the position we see that since we last took a census Black has gained two moves ; on the other hand he has lost in space, for White holds the centre more firmly than ever, and his Kt is strongly entrenched in a commanding position, and his B is well placed. Further, Black's K side has been badly weakened by the advance of the P's, and White's only weakness, his QRP, actually serves a useful purpose by stopping that combined advance of Black's Q side P majority, in which lies his only hope of saving the game. White's advantage is therefore pronounced.

26.	Q—Q2	Kt—B5
27.	P—KKt3	. . . . . .

You see now how important it is not to make P moves unnecessarily, or without deriving a real advantage from them. It is now clear enough that Black was wrong in moving his KKtP, but when he did it how could this be foreseen ? As a matter of fact his mistake was to take for a real attack what was no more than a simple diversion. His advantage being on the Q side, his aim should have been to threaten his opponent on the K side so as not to give him all the freedom but without weakening his own position.

27.	. . . . . .	Kt—R6 ch.
28.	K—Kt2	Kt × B
29.	R × Kt	. . . . . .

Again White threatens P—KR4. Black could meet the immediate threat by R—KKt1—Kt3, but White's reply of P × P and R—R1 would leave Black helpless, so he must look for another defence. He will defend his KtP with his K and his KRP with his R, so :

29.	. . . . . .	K—Kt3
30.	P—KR4	R—R1

White could now play 31 Kt × RP, and after 31 . . . . . ., R × Kt ; 32 P × P regain his piece, but then Black will hold the KR file, and though White has gained a P, his attack has come to an end, so he plays :

31.	P × P	P × P
32.	P—Q6 !	. . . . . .

The proper moment has arrived, and the passed pawn advances. Thus it ever is when a passed pawn is not blockaded. The pawn advances, not at a moment of your choosing, but when it suits your adversary, and you can never foretell the time of its advance ; you cannot make provision against it, the threat of it is ever over your head, and when it falls you are helpless against it. You will now not be astonished when you hear that an experienced player never leaves a passed pawn of his opponent's unblockaded.

33.	Q—Q2
34. Kt—K7 ch.	. . . . . .

You see by this that it was not with the idea of queening his P that White advanced it, but that it might support the Kt in his attack on the enemy King.

34.	K—Kt2
35. Q×P ch.	K—B1

White must here resist the temptation to take the Kt, for there would follow Q—R6 ch., and mate next move ! Even when you have a winning attack you must play with care and avoid falling into traps. Remember the example given in the Alekhin-Yates game (Diagram 14).

36. Kt—B5	. . . . . .

With the diagonal QB1—KR6 thus closed by White's Kt, which now protects the QP, Black is in great difficulties. White threatens two things, Q—Kt7 ch., and Q × Kt, and it would seem at first sight that his best defence would be Kt—R4 with the threat, if 37 R—R1, of 37 . . . . . ., Kt—B5 ch. ; 38 P × Kt, R—Kt1, but White has an answer in 39 R—R8 ! and after 39 . . . . . ., R × R, mates in two. Black therefore must seek another defence, and he plays :

36.	Kt—K1
37. R—R1	R × R

If Black had played here 37 . . . . . ., R—KKt1, a very beautiful mate in two would follow : 38

Q—K7 ch. ! Q×Q ; 39 P×Q mate. A veritable triumph for the passed pawn ! and a fine example of the distressful situation you may find yourself in, if you neglect to establish a firm blockade on a passed pawn.

38. K×R   ......

White now threatens R—R2 leading to another mate. In what follows Black's moves are forced. His position is hopeless.

38.	......	P—KB3
39.	Q—R6 ch.	K—B2
40.	Q—R7 ch.	K—K3
41.	Q—Kt8 ch.	Q—B2
42.	Kt—Kt7 ch.	Kt × Kt
43.	Q×R	......

And Black resigned, not only because of the loss of the exchange but because he is also threatened with the loss of his Q and with mate by Q—Q5 ch., etc. For he dare not take the QP since R—Q2 ch. would speedily force the issue. The passed pawn must therefore now queen. You will have noticed that the whole of White's attack, starting with 14 Kt—Q2, has had one aim, to add to the strength of the passed pawn, which in the end was the deciding element in Black's defeat.

Some of the variations in this game have been very pretty, but it is not on that account that I have discussed it in detail. The real reason is that it is very instructive as a study in the conflict of ideas, and as an example of Chess logic. Each party had formed a plan, in itself sound, based on an analysis of the position. If in the ensuing struggle one side got a decisive advantage, it was because he fathomed at the outset his opponent's idea and could make his plans accordingly, while his opponent failed to understand the full meaning of the attack he had to meet.   Hence in carrying out his plan he created weaknesses in his own camp of which the enemy could take advantage in developing his attack, and recognising his danger too late, no adequate defence could be found.

Do not, however, close this little book with the idea that if you analyse the position, and base a sound plan on your analysis, you will never lose a game !   You will lose many a game, but even in the games which you lose, your play will have been logical, and your opponent will have to go to great trouble to come out victorious.   If, however, you will follow carefully the ideas developed in this book, and avoid the many "don'ts" with which its pages are scattered, you will derive far greater pleasure from the game than you had before, for you will understand what precisely you are aiming at, and the motive behind each move and series of moves, and you will also understand your opponent's play, what his plan is, and you will realise that Chess is indeed a struggle between two minds, not a matter of chance, certainly not a mere haphazard moving of pieces, wood-shifting, as the great Blackburne called it.

Whether I have succeeded or not in my aim to explain to you how you must not play Chess, I hope that you will have learnt how to play the game. This will be a still greater thing : and then, looking back upon the days when you did not know how to play Chess, you will be able to say, after a well-earned victory, that now, at any rate, you really know

HOW NOT TO PLAY CHESS.

TEST YOURSELF QUIZ

by Fred Reinfeld

TEST YOURSELF QUIZ

by Fred Reinfeld

(Answers begin on page 102)

18 BLACK TO MOVE

What is White's threat and what can Black do about it?

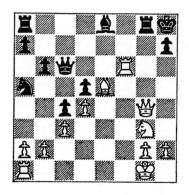

19 BLACK TO MOVE

Black's advanced Knight should move to . . . .

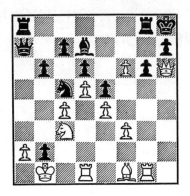

20   WHITE TO MOVE
Whose attack is stronger — White's or Black's?

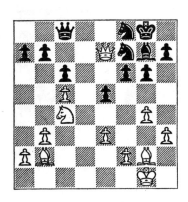

21   WHITE TO MOVE
Give White's strongest continuation.

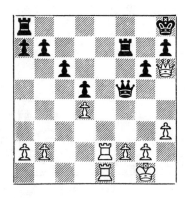

22   WHITE TO MOVE
What is White's advantage and how does he exploit it?

23 BLACK TO MOVE

Can Black avoid the threatened loss of a piece? How?

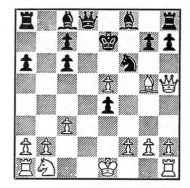

24 BLACK TO MOVE

Black played 1 ... Q—B2 and White replied ....

25 BLACK TO MOVE

How should Black meet the threatened loss of his Knight?

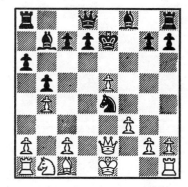

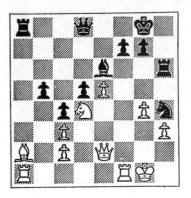

26 BLACK TO MOVE

What is the defect in White's position; can Black exploit it?

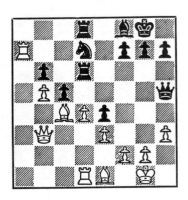

27 BLACK TO MOVE

If Black plays 1 . . . Kt —K4, how should White reply?

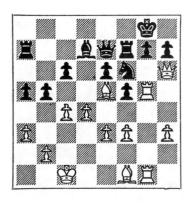

28 WHITE TO MOVE

Appraise this position and supply White's strongest line.

29 WHITE TO MOVE

What is Black's weak point? How does White proceed?

30 BLACK TO MOVE

What is White's weak point? How does Black exploit it?

31 WHITE TO MOVE

Should White play BxKt or guard his attacked Bishop?

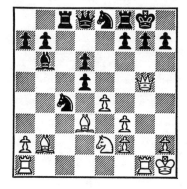

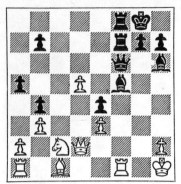

32 WHITE TO MOVE

Instead of playing 1 Kt —Q4, White resigned. Why?

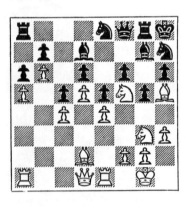

33 WHITE TO MOVE

Can White hope to win in this barricaded position?

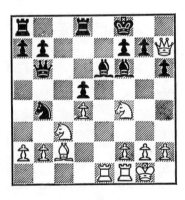

34 WHITE TO MOVE

What is White's most forcible continuation?

35 BLACK TO MOVE

Is 1 . . . P—KKt4 advisable to close the attacking lines?

36 BLACK TO MOVE

How does Black simplify to his advantage? Why?

37 WHITE TO MOVE

How does White set up a winning attack?

ANSWERS TO QUIZ

ANSWERS TO QUIZ

18　White threatens a fearful discovered check by moving his Rook from King Bishop 6. The most powerful Rook move would be R—B8 mate.

Black is powerless against this threat, for example 1 . . . RxQ; 2 R—B8 mate.

19　The strongest move by far is 1 . . . Kt—K6! winning White's Queen, for if 2 PxKt, Q—R5ch; 3 P—KKt3, QxKtP mate.

(White played the opening badly. The opening moves were 1 P—Q4, Kt—KB3; 2 Kt—Q2, P—K4; 3 PxP, Kt—Kt5; 4 P—KR3??)

20　At first glance this seems a very exciting fight, with White attacking the Black King on the King-side and Black attacking the White King on the Queen-side. But whereas White's Queen Rook Pawn is securely defended, Black is all too vulnerable on the other wing. The result is that White has a very pleasing finish:

　　　　　1 QxRPch!!　　　　KxQ
　　　　　2 R—R1ch　　　　　. . . .
The triumph of the open King Rook file.
　　　　　2 . . . .　　　　　B—R6
　　　　　3 RxB mate

When we re-examine the situation in Diagram 20, we see that Black's futile attacking gestures on the Queen-side actually had the damaging effect of removing his pieces from their proper defensive functions. For example, with Black's Queen at his King Bishop 2 square, this brilliant combination would have been impossible.

21   White has a distinct plus in mobility, and Black's pieces are huddled in a bleak defensive position. White can continue in strict positional style with 1 P—B4, but he has a much better line of play by setting up a Knight fork:

1 QxKt/B7ch!	KxKt
2 Kt—Q6ch	K moves
3 KtxQ	. . . .

With a piece ahead, White has an easy win.

22   White has a stranglehold on the open King file. By exploiting this open line he forces an immediate win:

1 R—K8ch	R—B1

On 1 . . . RxR there follows 2 RxRch, R—B1; 3 RxRch, QxR; 4 QxQ mate.

But after 1 . . . R—B1 it seems as if Black might hold the position, as capturing either Rook gets White nowhere; and 2 R/K8—K7 is satisfactorily answered by 2 . . . R—B2. But White has another way, which wins:

2 R/K1—K7!	. . . .

Black is helpless against the mate threat, as 2 . . . R—B2 is impossible and 2 . . . QxBPch; 3 K—R1 does not alter the situation.

23   White has sacrificed a piece for the attack, and it seems he must regain the piece. His threat is 1 PxKtch, PxP; 2 BxPch!, KxB; 3 Q—R4ch winning Black's Queen.

This looks terrifying, yet Black is far from despairing and calmly plays:

1 ....   Q—Q4!

Threatening . . . QxKP which would leave Black a piece ahead.

2 PxKtch   PxP

Now it turns out that White's Bishop is pinned — and cannot be saved. Thus Black remains a piece to the good. Black must be commended for not losing heart and finding a clever defence in what seemed a very bad position.

24   Black sees the threat 1 RxP, PxR; 2 BxP mate. Hence he plays:

1 ....   Q—B2??

Black's idea is that on 2 RxP? he will play 2 . . . QxQ; 3 PxQ, PxR; 4 BxPch, K—R1; 5 BxR, BxB and with a piece for two Pawns Black has an easy win. But Black has overlooked a much subtler threat:

2 QxPch!!   KxQ
3 BxP mate

Moral: in a defensive situation, don't assume that the threat you see is the only threat, or the strongest threat, available.

25   Black is momentarily a piece up for a Pawn. But his Knight is attacked and has no retreat. Nevertheless he can turn this seemingly precarious situation to his advantage by playing resourcefully:

| 1 .... | K—K1! |

The first point is that if White does not capture the Knight, Black saves this piece with . . . Kt—Kt4.

| 2 PxKt | Q—R5ch |

Now we see the second point: after 3 P—KKt3, QxKP; 4 QxQ, BxQ material is even, but Black's Bishops are all-powerful and he immediately wins a Pawn, leaving White's Pawn position in a shattered state. A fine example of inventive counterattack.

26 The fatal defect of White's game is that his Bishop has no scope and is permanently out of play; in effect, White is playing with a piece down.

Worse yet, the Bishop is subject to multiple attack — for example, by the doubling and even tripling of Black's heavy pieces on the Queen Rook file. The success of this manoeuvre is assured by the fact that White will be unable to move the Bishop out of the line of attack. What makes White's defensive prospects even more disheartening is that his Pawn position is riddled with weaknesses and his King's position is badly exposed. We have then the additional possibility that in some situations Black can even win by a quick switch to King-side attack. Play proceeds:

| 1 .... | R—R6! |

Already threatening to win the Bishop with 2 . . . Q—R4 or 2 . . . Q—R1.

| 2 Q—K1 | .... |

If White tries 2KtxP, Black continues 2 . . . Q—Kt3ch; 3 Kt—Q4, Q—R3 winning the unfortunate Bishop.

| 2 .... | Q—R4 |
| 3 Q—Kt1 | B—Q2 |

Another winning method is 3 . . . QxP; 4 Kt—K2, QxRP and White's game is hopeless.

After the text, the coming . . . R—R3 is absolutely decisive. The flexibility and mobility of Black's forces is in striking contrast to the lack of cooperation among White's pieces.

27   Black, feeling uncomfortable under the pressure of White's pieces, wants to free himself somewhat by driving back White's King Bishop. Hence:

| 1 . . . . | Kt—K4? |

Black thinks this move is playable because after 2 PxKt he can avoid the loss of a piece. But, as the sequel will demonstrate, Black has not looked ahead far enough.

| 2 PxKt! | QxR |

The only way to recapture, as 2 . . . RxR?? is disastrous because of 3 BxPch winning the Queen.

| 3 PxR | QxBch |

Apparently White was under the impression that the reply 4 K—R2? is now forced, whereupon 4 . . . BxPch wins for Black.

| 4 B—B1! | . . . . |

But this quiet interposition wins for White, for after 4 . . . BxP?; 5 QxPch leads to mate on the following move. And 4 . . . RxP? leads to the same result.

The disagreeable consequence for Black is that he is confronted with a menacing, far-advanced passed Pawn and threats of checkmate.

4	K—R1
5 QxP	Q—Q8
6 P—Q7	Q—Q3
7 P—Kt3	P—R3

if he is to be successful in turning his advantage to
account.

1 K—Kt2!   ....

Now White really threatens 2 KtxP, KtxKt; 3 BxKt,
BxB; 4 RxB, RxR; 5 QxR, as Black no longer has a
check available.

1 ....   Q—K4

This defence of the Pawn proves inadequate, but 1
. . . Q—B3 is not much better. White then continues
2 B—Q1! followed by 3 B—Kt3 and 4 P—B4! with a
view to P—B5, driving Black's Bishop away from the
defence of the Queen Pawn.

2 P—Kt4!   ....

Forcing Black's Rook to give up the defence of the
Queen Pawn.

2 ....   R—B5

Black hopes for 3 KtxP, RxR; 4 PxR?, KtxKt!;
5 PxQ, Kt—B5ch followed by 6 . . . KtxQ and Black
is a piece ahead.

3 KtxP!   ....

Is White falling into the trap? No, for he has a
winning finesse in mind.

3 ....   BxKt

Black changes his mind, for he sees that on 3 . . .
RxR White will interpolate 4 KtxKtch!, QxKt; 5 PxR
and White has safely won a Pawn.

4 RxB!   R—B6

Or 4 . . . KtxR; 5 QxR, Kt—Kt3; 6 Q—K4! and
White wins a second Pawn.

5 RxQ   RxQ
6 R—R5!   ....

And now White wins a second Pawn, as Black cannot simultaneously defend his Queen Knight Pawn
and Queen Rook Pawn. Thus White has carefully

and ably carried out his plan. In the foregoing play we have a good example of the tactical skill which is often required to exploit a strategical advantage.

30 Here White's weakness is his backward Queen Bishop Pawn. This unfortunate Pawn cannot be guarded by Pawns, nor can it be advanced or exchanged. It therefore forms a perfect target for pressure by Black's Rooks.

However, if White is given the necessary time, he will play Kt–Kt2 followed by Kt–B4, successfully masking any further attack on his weak Pawn. Black must therefore lose no time in driving his advantage home.

1 ....   Q–B4!

Threatening 2 . . . QxQ which would win a piece.

2 R–K4   ....

It is clear that 2 Kt–Kt2 loses the Pawn at once (2 . . . RxP!; 3 RxR, RxR; 4 RxKt, QxQ; 5 R–K8ch, B–B1; 6 KtxQ, RxB etc.); while after 2 QxQ, KtxQ, the weak Pawn likewise falls.

2 ....   Kt–Q4!

Just in time to prevent White from carrying out the contemplated manoeuvre Kt–Kt2–B4.

3 Kt–Kt2   Kt–B6!

Now White is forced to capture the intruder, for if 4 R/K4–K1?, QxQ wins for Black — for example 5 KtxQ, Kt–R7 winning the weak Pawn; or 5 PxQ, Kt–K7ch winning the Exchange.

4 BxKt   RxB
5 Q–K2   B–R3!

The real point of Black's Knight manoeuvre to force the disappearance of White's Bishop. Now Black drives off the defending Rook and thus finally wins the weak Pawn.

6 R—K8ch	RxR
7 QxRch	K—Kt2
8 R—B1	RxBP

And White wins easily in the endgame. As was the case in Diagram 29, pressure on a positional weakness favored the player with the more aggressive development.

31   White has much more ambitious plans than playing a trite move such as BxKt. The point is that he has a magnificent attacking position along the King Knight file, supported by the powerful Bishop striking along the long diagonal. If Black is given the opportunity, he will exchange Queens, bringing the attack to an abrupt end. So White must act quickly.

1 QxKtPch!!	KtxQ
2 RxKtch	K—R1
3 R—Kt8 dbl ch!!	. . . .

The point of White's sacrifice.

3	KxR
4 R—KKtlch	Q—Kt4
5 RxQ mate	

Call this inspiration if you will; but it represents the flawless fusing together of elements that are subject to analysis. If White realises the value of the concentrated pressure against King Knight 7, he is halfway on the road to this beautiful combination.

32   White resigned because he realized that 1 Kt—Q4 would be answered by 1 . . . B—R6!! leaving White defenceless.

However, this "answer" only increases the mystery of White's resignation, so let us examine the position of Diagram 32 in some detail. It soon becomes clear that Black has an enormous advantage. He has completed his development, whereas White's Queen Rook and Queen Bishop are still on their home squares and absolutely useless.

Secondly, we observe that while Black's King is quite safe, White's King is in danger because several protective Pawns have disappeared. Add these factors: Black's Bishops have considerable scope, and the tripling of his heavy pieces on the King Bishop file looks menacing. But the question remains why White did not at least try 1 Kt—Q4. This is what would have happened:

1 Kt—Q4	B—R6!!

Although this move is astonishing at first glance, there is enormous power behind it. Black's threats are so powerful that he will be able to win quickly even if his Queen is captured.

2 RxQ	RxR

Threatening . . . R—B8 mate. And if 3 B—Kt2, R—B8ch; 4 RxR, RxR mate. So White tries a different way.

3 Kt—K2	R—B8ch
4 Kt—Kt1	RxKtch
5 KxR	R—B8 mate

It is the overwhelming superiority of Black's development that makes his drastic victory possible. Black's superiority prevails even when White declines the sacrifice. Let us return to Diagram 32 and try another way for White:

1 Kt—Q4	B—R6!!
2 R—KKt1	Q—R5

              3 B—Kt2   ....

Too late. Black now infiltrates decisively into
White's fatally weakened castled position.

              3 ....   R—B7
              4 Q—K1   B—B8

And Black mates shortly.

33   Black's position is so constricted that he hardly
has any moves left. Yet the Pawn position is so
blockaded that it seems difficult if not impossible for
White to make any headway.

Still, it does not take White long to evolve a
highly ingenious winning plan. This has two parts: (1)
to sacrifice his Knight on King Bishop 5 for Black's
Queen Pawn, which will make it possible to win
Black's Queen Bishop Pawn; (2) to follow this up
with the advance of his own Queen Bishop Pawn to
Bishop 6. Given the slight mobility of Black's pieces,
he will be helpless against the "Pawnroller."

In preparation for the first step, White brings his
Bishop to King 3 and his Queen to Queen Rook 3.
In preparation for the second step, White places his
Rooks on Queen Bishop 1 and Queen 1, where they
will be most effective in supporting the intended
Pawn advance. The whole plan proceeds like clock-
work.

              1 Q—B1!   R—Q1
              2 Q—R3   B—B1
              3 B—K3   R—Q2
              4 QR—B1   R—Q1
              5 KR—Q1   B—Q2

Now White is ready for the sacrifice.

              6 KtxQP!   KtxKt

The alternative 6 . . . QxKt; 7 BxBP, Q—Kt1; 8

B—K7, QR—B1; 9 P—B5 is just as bad for Black, as White carries out the plan outlined above.

7	BxBP	B—B1
8	B—KKt4!	....

This removes an important defensive piece and thus lends added strength to the intensification of the pin by Kt—B5.

8	....	BxB
9	PxB	R—Q2
10	Kt—B5	Q—Q1
11	BxKt	....

Now that White has recovered the sacrificed piece and is two Pawns ahead, he has an easy win.

11	....	Kt—B1
12	P—B5	Kt—Kt3
13	P—B6	PxP
14	PxP	RxB

Black's despair is justified. If 14 . . . R—KB2; 15 P—Kt7 and the Pawn queens.

15	QxR	QxQ
16	RxQ	Resigns

There is nothing to be done against the advance of the passed Pawns. An impressive example of the value of a carefully considered plan; such plans are almost magical in the effective way they dispose of obstacles.

34 With Black's King driven from the castled position, White has an overwhelming attack, with several winning lines at his disposal.

The simplest method would be 1 B—Kt3, with a view to 2 P—QR3 followed by 3 Kt/B3xP, BxKt; 4 Q—R8 mate. If Black answers 1 B—Kt3 with 1 . . .

QxP, White can reply 2 RxB, PxR; 3 KtxKPch winning the Queen — or 2 RxB, QxKt/B5; 3 Q—R8 mate.

Now that we see the dangers to which Black's King is exposed, we can try a more complicated method: 1 Kt/B3xP!, KtxKt (not 1 . . . BxKt; 2 Q—R8 mate); 2 KtxKt, RxKt; 3 Q—R8ch, K—K2; 4 QxR. This is certainly good enough to win for White, but he has an even more convincing line:

| 1 P—QR3! | .... |

Very strong — the idea is to force Black's Knight to give up the protection of his Queen Pawn.

| 1 .... | KtxB |
| 2 Kt/B3xP! | RxKt |

If 2 . . . BxKt; 3 Q—R8 mate.

| 3 KtxR | Resigns |

Black is helpless, as his Queen is attacked, Q—R8 mate is threatened, and 3 . . . BxKt allows 4 Q—R8 mate. It is always instructive to see how a good player seeks the simplest, most convincing road to victory.

35   Before considering the merits of 1 . . . P—KKt4, we have to get our bearings. White has a huge plus in mobility, as Black's pieces are huddled together and have very little scope. Furthermore, we note that Black's King-side has been weakened by the advance of his King Rook Pawn and King Knight Pawn, and that in consequence White has advanced *his* King Rook Pawn in order to open the King Rook file. Black, on the other hand, has no similar target for attack on the other wing.

Finally, note that White has five pieces on hand to menace the Black King, whereas Black has no threats against the White King. When we sum up

all these factors, we realise that the chances are that
White can refute 1 . . . P–KKt4. Let us see:

1	P–KKt4

The object of this move is to prevent White from
opening the King Rook file. But, thanks to the advantages previously outlined, White can sacrifice
successfully.

2 Kt/K4xKtP!	. . . .

This threatens Q–R7 mate.

2	PxKt
3 P–R6!	. . . .

Black cannot capture the Bishop, for if 3 . . . PxB;
4 PxB dbl ch, KxP; 5 Q–R7 mate (or 5 R–R7 mate).

3	BxRP
4 BxP	K–Kt2
5 BxBch	KtxB
6 RxKt!	KxR
7 R–R1ch	. . . .

And White mates next move. Thus we see that 1
. . . P–KKt4 would not have achieved its objective
of closing the King Rook file; White's margin of
extra mobility is much too great to give Black a
chance to escape.

Returning to Diagram 35, let us follow the course
of the actual play, which makes a fine study in incisive
middle-game tactics.

1	QPxP
2 QPxP	P–QKt4
3 BPxP	QxKtP
4 PxP	PxP

White has attained his objective — the opening of
the King Rook file. But now he is confronted with a
crisis: both his Bishop and his King Pawn are attacked.
He solves the difficulty very cleverly.

	5 Kt—R4!	. . . .

Very tricky. Black cannot play 5 . . . RxB because of 6 KtxPch, K—R2; 7 Kt—Kt5 mate. Nor will 5 . . . P—KKt4 do because of 6 Kt—Kt6ch, K—R2; 7 KtxKtP mate. And on 5 . . . K—R2 there are various winning methods, for example 6 KtxP! or 6 Kt—Kt5ch!

	5		KtxP

Black gives up the Exchange to gain some relief that proves only temporary.

6 BxKt	BxB
7 KtxPch	K—Kt2
8 KtxR	RxKt
9 R—R3!	. . . .

Generally, when a player with an aggressive position wins some material his attack slows down. This is not the case here, because White's pieces are placed to very good advantage.

9	Kt—B3
10 R—QKt3	Q—R3

Or 10 . . . Q—K1; 11 Q—B5 and White has a winning attack.

11 Kt—B5	Q—B3
12 R—K1!	Resigns

A curious position. If 12 . . . B—Q3; 13 Kt—K6ch or 12 . . . Q—Q3; 13 R—Q3, B—Q5; 14 RxB, QxR; 15 Kt—K6ch and in either case White wins the Queen.

A convincing demonstration of the value of open lines. White drove his advantage home relentlessly by stressing his superior mobility.

36 A player who is ahead in material finds that simplifying exchanges ease the problem of making his material advantage tell in his favor. The fewer pieces left on the board, the less opportunity his opponent has to create diversions and complications that might becloud the issue.

Acting on this principle, Black, who is the Exchange ahead, wants to simplify. In this case this involves the exchange of Queens. The method selected is subtle and forceful.

| | 1 .... | Q—K5! |

Very ingenious. The answer to 2 BxQ is 2 . . . Kt—K7ch; 3 K—B1, KtxQch. Now White cannot play 4 K—Kt1 because of 4 . . . R—R8 mate. Hence he must play 4 K—K1, leading to 4 . . . R—R8ch; 5 K—Q2, KtxBch and Black is a whole Rook ahead.

Obviously 2 BxQ won't do, but meanwhile Black is threatening to win outright with . . . Q—R2.

| | 2 QxKt | .... |

Reluctantly White decides to simplify, as he sees that 2 B—Q1 will not do because of 2 . . . Q—R2; 3 P—B3, R—R8ch; 4 K—B2, Kt—Q6ch etc.

| | 2 .... | QxQ |
| | 3 BxQ | RxB |

Now Black has obtained the exchanges he wanted. White's weak Queen-side Pawns make vulnerable targets.

| | 4 R—K1 | R—QR5! |

Black will win the ending without much trouble. Black's procedure is an instructive example of how to use powerful threats to bring about a simplified endgame.

37 Most players with the White pieces would automatically remove the attacked Rook. But instead of this mechanical retreat White finds a brilliant surprise attack:

| | 1 B—K4!! | .... |

Threatening 2 QxRP mate. If Black tries 1 . . . P–Kt3, the continuation is 2 B–B6! (threatens Q–R6 and mate), KtxR (if 2 . . . P–KR4; 3 RxP wins); 3 BxKt, P–KR4 (if 3 . . . BxB; 4 Q–R6 forces mate); 4 B–QB3! (threatening Q–B6 followed by mate), K–R2 (if 4 . . . Q–Q1; 5 Q–Q4! forces mate); 5 Q–B6, R–KKt1; 6 QxBPch, K–R3; 7 BxB and wins.

Likewise 1 . . . P–KR3 leads to a lost game after 2 BxP. Black cannot reply 2 . . . PxB because of 3 R–KKt5ch! forcing mate. If he tries 2 . . . P–B4 there follows 3 Q–Kt5, Q–B2; 4 BxKtP!, QxB; 5 QxQch, KxQ; 6 R–Q7ch. White recovers the piece and remains with a considerable material advantage.

1	P–B4
2 BxP!	RxB
3 R–Q8ch	QxR
4 BxQ and wins	

White's substantial material advantage gives him an easy win.

Sudden attacks of this kind can often upset the most carefully laid plans. This is especially so when a Queen is separated from the defence, as is the case here.

CATALOGUE OF DOVER BOOKS

Chess, Checkers, Games, Go

THE ADVENTURE OF CHESS, Edward Lasker. A lively history of chess, from its ancient beginnings in the Indian 4-handed game of Chaturanga, through to the great players of our day, as told by one of America's finest masters. He introduces such unusual sidelights and amusing oddities as Maelzel's chess-playing automaton that beat Napoleon 3 times. Major discussion of chess-playing machines and personal memories of Nimzovich, Capablanca, etc. 5-page chess primer. 11 illustrations, 53 diagrams. 296pp. 5⅜ x 8.   S510 Paperbound **$1.75**

A TREASURY OF CHESS LORE, edited by Fred Reinfeld. A delightful collection of anecdotes, short stories, aphorisms by and about the masters, poems, accounts of games and tournaments, photography. Hundreds of humorous, pithy, satirical, wise, and historical episodes, comments, and word portraits. A fascinating "must" for chess players; revealing and perhaps seductive to those who wonder what their friends see in the game. 48 photographs (14 full page plates) 12 diagrams. xi + 306pp. 5⅜ x 8.   T458 Paperbound **$1.75**

HOW DO YOU PLAY CHESS? by Fred Reinfeld. A prominent expert covers every basic rule of chess for the beginner in 86 questions and answers: moves, powers of pieces, rationale behind moves, how to play forcefully, history of chess, and much more. Bibliography of chess publications. 11 board diagrams. 48 pages.   **FREE**

THE PLEASURES OF CHESS, Assiac. Internationally known British writer, influential chess columnist, writes wittily about wide variety of chess subjects: Anderssen's "Immortal Game;" only game in which both opponents resigned at once; psychological tactics of Reshevsky, Lasker; varieties played by masters for relaxation, such as "losing chess;" sacrificial orgies; etc. These anecdotes, witty observations will give you fresh appreciation of game. 43 problems. 150 diagrams. 139pp. 5⅜ x 8.   T597 Paperbound **$1.25**

WIN AT CHESS, F. Reinfeld. 300 practical chess situations from actual tournament play to sharpen your chess eye and test your skill. Traps, sacrifices, mates, winning combinations, subtle exchanges, show you how to WIN AT CHESS. Short notes and tables of solutions and alternative moves help you evaluate your progress. Learn to think ahead playing the "crucial moments" of historic games. 300 diagrams. Notes and solutions. Formerly titled CHESS QUIZ. vi + 120pp. 5⅜ x 8.   T438 Paperbound **$1.00**

THE ART OF CHESS, James Mason. An unabridged reprinting of the latest revised edition of the most famous general study of chess ever written. Also included, a complete supplement by Fred Reinfeld, "How Do You Play Chess?", invaluable to beginners for its lively question and answer method. Mason, an early 20th century master, teaches the beginning and intermediate player more than 90 openings, middle game, end game, how to see more moves ahead, to plan purposefully, attack, sacrifice, defend, exchange, and govern general strategy. Supplement. 448 diagrams. 1947 Reinfeld-Bernstein text. Bibliography. xvi + 340pp. 5⅜ x 8.   T463 Paperbound **$2.00**

THE PRINCIPLES OF CHESS, James Mason. This "great chess classic" (N. Y. Times) is a general study covering all aspects of the game: basic forces, resistance, obstruction, opposition, relative values, mating, typical end game situations, combinations, much more. The last section discusses openings, with 50 games illustrating modern master play of Rubinstein, Spielmann, Lasker, Capablanca, etc., selected and annotated by Fred Reinfeld. Will improve the game of any intermediate-skilled player, but is so forceful and lucid that an absolute beginner might use it to become an accomplished player. 1946 Reinfeld edition. 166 diagrams. 378pp. 5⅜ x 8.   T646 Paperbound **$1.85**

LASKER'S MANUAL OF CHESS, Dr. Emanuel Lasker. Probably the greatest chess player of modern times, Dr. Emanuel Lasker held the world championship 28 years, independent of passing schools or fashions. This unmatched study of the game, chiefly for intermediate to skilled players, analyzes basic methods, combinations, position play, the aesthetics of chess, dozens of different openings, etc., with constant reference to great modern games. Contains a brilliant exposition of Steinitz's important theories. Introduction by Fred Reinfeld. Tables of Lasker's tournament record. 3 indices. 308 diagrams. 1 photograph. xxx + 349pp. 5⅜ x 8.   T640 Paperbound **$2.25**

THE ART OF CHESS COMBINATION, E. Znosko-Borovsky. Proves that combinations, perhaps the most aesthetically satisfying, successful technique in chess, can be an integral part of your game, instead of a haphazard occurrence. Games of Capablanca, Rubinstein, Nimzovich, Bird, etc. grouped according to common features, perceptively analyzed to show that every combination begins in certain simple ideas. Will help you to plan many moves ahead. Technical terms almost completely avoided. "In the teaching of chess he may claim to have no superior," P. W. Sergeant. Introduction. Exercises. Solutions. Index. 223pp. 5⅜ x 8.   T583 Paperbound **$1.60**

MODERN IDEAS IN CHESS, Richard Reti. An enduring classic, because of its unrivalled explanation of the way master chess had developed in the past hundred years. Reti, who was an outstanding theoretician and player, explains each advance in chess by concentrating on the games of the single master most closely associated with it: Morphy, Anderssen, Steinitz, Lasker, Alekhine, other world champions. Play the games in this volume, study Reti's perceptive observations, and have a living picture of the road chess has travelled. Introduction. 34 diagrams. 192pp. 5⅜ x 8.　　　　　　　　　　　　　　　　T638 Paperbound **$1.25**

THE BOOK OF THE NEW YORK INTERNATIONAL CHESS TOURNAMENT, 1924, annotated by A. Alekhine and edited by H. Helms. Long a rare collector's item, this is the book of one of the most brilliant tournaments of all time, during which Capablanca, Lasker, Alekhine, Reti, and others immeasurably enriched chess theory in a thrilling contest. All 110 games played, with Alekhine's unusually penetrating notes. 15 photographs. xi + 271pp. 5⅜ x 8.
T752 Paperbound **$1.85**

KERES' BEST GAMES OF CHESS, selected, annotated by F. Reinfeld. 90 best games, 1931-1948, by one of boldest, most exciting players of modern chess. Games against Alekhine, Bogolyubov, Capablanca, Euwe, Fine, Reshevsky, other masters, show his treatments of openings such as Giuoco Piano, Alekhine Defense, Queen's Gambit Declined; attacks, sacrifices, alternative methods. Preface by Keres gives personal glimpses, evaluations of rivals. 110 diagrams. 272pp. 5⅜ x 8.　　　　　　　　　　　　　　　　T593 Paperbound **$1.35**

HYPERMODERN CHESS as developed in the games of its greatest exponent, ARON NIMZOVICH, edited by Fred Reinfeld. An intensely original player and analyst, Nimzovich's extraordinary approaches startled and often angered the chess world. This volume, designed for the average player, shows in his victories over Alekhine, Lasker, Marshall, Rubinstein, Spielmann, and others, how his iconoclastic methods infused new life into the game. Use Nimzovich to invigorate your play and startle opponents. Introduction. Indices of players and openings. 180 diagrams. viii + 220pp. 5⅜ x 8.　　　　　　　　　　　T448 Paperbound **$1.50**

THE DEVELOPMENT OF A CHESS GENIUS: 100 INSTRUCTIVE GAMES OF ALEKHINE, F. Reinfeld. 100 games of the chess giant's formative years, 1905-1914, from age 13 to maturity, each annotated and commented upon by Fred Reinfeld. Included are matches against Bogolyubov, Capablanca, Tarrasch, and many others. You see the growth of an inexperienced genius into one of the greatest players of all time. Many of these games have never appeared before in book form. "One of America's most significant contributions to the chess world," Chess Life. New introduction. Index of players, openings. 204 illustrations. xv +227pp. 5¾ x 8.
T551 Paperbound **$1.35**

RESHEVSKY'S BEST GAMES OF CHESS, Samuel Reshevsky. One time 4-year-old chess genius, 5-time winner U. S. Chess Championship, selects, annotates 110 of his best games, illustrating theories, favorite methods of play against Capablanca, Alekhine, Bogolyubov, Kashdan, Vidmar, Botvinnik, others. Clear, non-technical style. Personal impressions of opponents, autobiographical material, tournament match record. Formerly "Reshevsky on Chess." 309 diagrams, 2 photos. 288pp. 5⅜ x 8.　　　　　　　　　　　　　　　T606 Paperbound **$1.25**

ONE HUNDRED SELECTED GAMES, Mikhail Botvinnik. Author's own choice of his best games before becoming World Champion in 1948, beginning with first big tournament, the USSR Championship, 1927. Shows his great power of analysis as he annotates these games, giving strategy, technique against Alekhine, Capablanca, Euwe, Keres, Reshevsky, Smyslov, Vidmar, many others. Discusses his career, methods of play, system of training. 6 studies of endgame positions. 221 diagrams. 272pp. 5⅜ x 8.　　　　　　　　　　T620 Paperbound **$1.50**

RUBINSTEIN'S CHESS MASTERPIECES, selected, annotated by Hans Kmoch. Thoroughgoing mastery of opening, middle game; faultless technique in endgame, particularly rook and pawn endings; ability to switch from careful positional play to daring combinations; all distinguish the play of Rubinstein. 100 best games, against Janowski, Nimzowitch, Tarrasch, Vidmar, Capablanca, other greats, carefully annotated, will improve your game rapidly. Biographical introduction, B. F. Winkelman. 103 diagrams. 192pp. 5⅜ x 8.
T617 Paperbound **$1.25**

TARRASCH'S BEST GAMES OF CHESS, selected & annotated by Fred Reinfeld. First definitive collection of games by Siegbert Tarrasch, winner of 7 international tournaments, and the leading theorist of classical chess. 183 games cover fifty years of play against Mason, Mieses, Paulsen, Teichmann, Pillsbury, Janwoski, others. Reinfeld includes Tarrasch's own analyses of many of these games. A careful study and replaying of the games will give you a sound understanding of classical methods, and many hours of enjoyment. Introduction. Indexes. 183 diagrams. xxiv + 386pp. 5⅜ x 8.　　　　　　　T644 Paperbound **$2.00**

MARSHALL'S BEST GAMES OF CHESS, F. J. Marshall. Grandmaster, U. S. Champion for 27 years, tells story of career; presents magnificent collection of 140 of best games, annotated by himself. Games against Alekhine, Capablanca, Emanuel Lasker, Janowski, Rubinstein, Pillsbury, etc. Special section analyzes openings such as King's Gambit, Ruy Lopez, Alekhine's Defense, Giuoco Piano, others. A study of Marshall's brilliant offensives, slashing attacks, extraordinary sacrifices, will rapidly improve your game. Formerly "My Fifty Years of Chess." Introduction. 19 diagrams. 13 photos. 250pp. 5⅜ x 8.　　　　　　T604 Paperbound **$1.45**

THE HASTINGS CHESS TOURNAMENT, 1895, edited by Horace F. Cheshire. This is the complete tournament book of the famous Hastings 1895 tournament. One of the most exciting tournaments ever to take place, it evoked the finest play from such players as Dr. Lasker, Steinitz, Tarrasch, Harry Pillsbury, Mason, Tchigorin, Schlecter, and others. It was not only extremely exciting as an event, it also created first-rate chess. This book contains fully annotated all 230 games, full information about the playing events, biographies of the players, and much other material that makes it a chess classic. 22 photos, 174 diagrams. x + 370pp. 5⅝ x 8½. **T288 Paperbound $2.00**

THE BOOK OF THE NOTTINGHAM INTERNATIONAL CHESS TOURNAMENT, 1936, Annotated by Dr. Alexander Alekhine. The Nottingham 1936 tournament is regarded by many chess enthusiasts as the greatest tournament of recent years. It brought together all the living former world champions, the current chess champion, and the future world champion: Dr. Lasker, Capablanca, Alekhine, Euwe, Botvinnik, and Reshevsky, Fine, Flohr, Tartakover, Vidmar, and Bogoljubov. The play was brilliant throughout. This volume contains all 105 of the games played, provided with the remarkable annotations of Alekhine. 1 illustration, 121 diagrams. xx + 291pp. 5⅜ x 8½. **T189 Paperbound $2.00**

CHESS FOR FUN AND CHESS FOR BLOOD, Edward Lasker. A genial, informative book by one of century's leading masters. Incisive comments on chess as a form of art and recreation, on how a master prepares for and plays a tournament. Best of all is author's move-by-move analysis of his game with Dr. Emanuel Lasker in 1924 World Tournament, a charming and thorough recreation of one of the great games in history: the author's mental processes; how his calculations were upset; how both players blundered; the surprising outcome. Who could not profit from this study-in-depth? For the enthusiast who likes to read about chess as well as play it. Corrected (1942) edition. Preface contains 8 letters to author about the fun of chess. 95 illustrations by Maximilian Mopp. 224pp. 5⅜ x 8½. **T146 Paperbound $1.25**

HOW NOT TO PLAY CHESS, Eugene A. Znosko-Borovsky. Sticking to a few well-chosen examples and explaining every step along the way, an outstanding chess expositor shows how to avoid playing a hit-or-miss game and instead develop general plans of action based on positional analysis: weak and strong squares, the notion of the controlled square, how to seize control of open lines, weak points in the pawn structure, and so on. Definition and illustration of typical chess mistakes plus 20 problems (from master games) added by Fred Reinfeld for the 1949 edition and a number of good-to-memorize tips make this a lucid book that can teach in a few hours what might otherwise take years to learn. 119pp. 5⅜ x 8. **T920 Paperbound $1.00**

THE SOVIET SCHOOL OF CHESS, A. Kotov and M. Yudovich. 128 master games, most unavailable elsewhere, by 51 outstanding players, including Botvinnik, Keres, Smyslov, Tal, against players like Capablanca, Euwe, Reshevsky. All carefully annotated, analyzed. Valuable biographical information about each player, early history of Russian chess, careers and contributions of Chigorin and Alekhine, development of Soviet school from 1920 to present with full over-all study of main features of its games, history of Russian chess literature. The most comprehensive work on Russian chess ever printed, the richest single sourcebook for up-to-date Russian theory and strategy. New introduction. Appendix of Russian Grandmasters, Masters, Master Composers. Two indexes (Players, Games). 30 photographs. 182 diagrams. vi + 390pp. 5⅜ x 8. **T26 Paperbound $2.00**

THE ART OF THE CHECKMATE, Georges Renaud and Victor Kahn. Two former national chess champions of France examine 127 games, identify 23 kinds of mate, and show the rationale for each. These include Legal's pseudo sacrifice, the double check, the smothered mate, Greco's mate, Morphy's mate, the mate of two bishops, two knights, many, many more. Analysis of ideas, not memorization problems. Review quizzes with answers help readers gauge progress. 80 quiz examples and solutions. 299 diagrams. vi + 208pp. **T106 Paperbound $1.35**

HOW TO SOLVE CHESS PROBLEMS, K. S. Howard. Full of practical suggestions for the fan or the beginner—who knows only the moves of the chessmen. Contains preliminary section and 58 two-move, 46 three-move, and 8 four-move problems composed by 27 outstanding American problem creators in the last 30 years. Explanation of all terms and exhaustive index. "Just what is wanted for the student," Brian Harley. 112 problems, solutions. vi +171pp. 5⅜ x 8. **T748 Paperbound $1.00**

CHESS STRATEGY, Edward Lasker. Keres, Fine, and other great players have acknowledged their debt to this book, which has taught just about the whole modern school how to play forcefully and intelligently. Covers fundamentals, general strategic principles, middle and end game, objects of attack, etc. Includes 48 dramatic games from master tournaments, all fully analyzed. "Best textbook I know in English," J. R. Capablanca. New introduction by author. Table of openings. Index. 167 illustrations. vii + 282pp. 5⅜ x 8. **T528 Paperbound $1.65**

REINFELD ON THE END GAME IN CHESS, F. Reinfeld. Formerly titled PRACTICAL END-GAME PLAY, this book contains clear, simple analyses of 62 end games by such masters as Alekhine, Tarrasch, Marshall, Morphy, Capablanca, and many others. Primary emphasis is on the general principles of transition from middle play to end play. This book is unusual in analyzing weak or incorrect moves to show how error occurs and how to avoid it. Covers king and pawn, minor piece, queen endings, weak squares, centralization, tempo moves, and many other vital factors. 62 diagrams. vi + 177pp. 5⅜ x 8. **T417 Paperbound $1.25**

THE AMERICAN TWO-MOVE CHESS PROBLEM, Kenneth S. Howard. One of this country's foremost contemporary problem composers selects an interesting, diversified collection of the best two-movers by 58 top American composers. Involving complete blocks, mutates, line openings and closings, other unusual moves, these problems will help almost any player improve his strategic approach. Probably has no equal for all around artistic excellence, surprising keymoves, interesting strategy. Includes 30-page history of development of American two-mover from Loyd, its founder, to the present. Index of composers. vii + 99pp. 5⅜ x 8½.
T997 Paperbound **$1.00**

WIN AT CHECKERS, M. Hopper. (Formerly CHECKERS). The former World's Unrestricted Checker Champion discusses the principles cf the game, expert's shots and traps, problems for the beginner, standard openings, locating your best move, the end game, opening "blitzkrieg" moves, ways to draw when you are behind your opponent, etc. More than 100 detailed questions and answers anticipate your problems. Appendix. 75 problems with solutions and diagrams. Index. 79 figures. xi + 107pp. 5⅜ x 8. T363 Paperbound **$1.00**

GAMES ANCIENT AND ORIENTAL, AND HOW TO PLAY THEM, E. Falkener. A connoisseur's selection of exciting and different games: Oriental varieties of chess, with unusual pieces and moves (including Japanese shogi); the original pachisi; go; reconstructions of lost Roman and Egyptian games; and many more. Full rules and sample games. Now play at home the games that have entertained millions, not on a fad basis, but for millennia. 345 illustrations and figures. iv + 366pp. 5⅜ x 8. T739 Paperbound **$2.00**

GO AND GO-MOKU, Edward Lasker. A fascinating Oriental game, Go, is winning new devotees in America daily. Rules that you can learn in a few minutes—a wealth of combinations that makes it more profound than chess! This is an easily followed step-by-step explanation of this 2000-year-old game, beginning with fundamentals. New chapter on advanced strategy in this edition! Also contains rules for Go-Moku, a very easy sister game. 72 diagrams. xix + 215pp. 5⅜ x 8. T613 Paperbound **$1.50**

HOW TO FORCE CHECKMATE, F. Reinfeld. Formerly titled CHALLENGE TO CHESSPLAYERS, this is an invaluable collection of 300 lightning strokes selected from actual masters' play, which will demonstrate how to smash your opponent's game with strong decisive moves. No board needed — clear, practical diagrams and easy-to-understand solutions. Learn to plan up to three moves ahead and play a superior end game. 300 diagrams. 111pp. 5⅜ x 8.
T439 Paperbound **$1.25**

CHESSBOARD MAGIC! A COLLECTION OF 160 BRILLIANT ENDINGS, I. Cherney. Contains 160 endgame compositions, all illustrating not only ingenuity of composition, but inherent beauty of solution. In one, five Knights are needed to force mate; in another White forces stalemate though Black finishes eight passed pawns ahead; 150 more, all remarkable, all will sharpen your imagination and increase your skill. "Inexhaustible source of entertainment, an endless feast of delight," Reuben Fine, Grandmaster. Introduction. 160 diagrams. Index of composers. vii + 172pp. 5⅜ x 8. T607 Paperbound **$1.00**

LEARN CHESS FROM THE MASTERS, F. Reinfeld. Formerly titled CHESS BY YOURSELF, this book contains 10 games which you play against such masters as Marshall, Bronstein, Najdorf, and others, and an easy system for grading each move you make against a variety of other possible moves. Detailed annotations reveal the principles of the game through actual play. 91 diagrams. viii + 144pp. 5⅜ x 8. T362 Paperbound **$1.00**

MORPHY'S GAMES OF CHESS, edited by Philip W. Sergeant. You can put boldness into your game by following the brilliant, forceful moves of the man who has been called the greatest chess player of all time. Here are 300 of Morphy's best games carefully annotated to reveal Morphy's principles. 54 classics against masters like Anderssen, Harrwitz, Bird, Paulsen, and others. 52 games at odds; 54 blindfold games; plus over 100 others. Unabridged reissue of the latest revised edition. Bibliography. New introduction by Fred Reinfeld. Annotations and introduction by Sergeant. Index. 235 diagrams. x + 352pp. 5⅜ x 8. T386 Paperbound **$1.85**

CHESS PRAXIS, Aron Nimzovich. Nimzovich was the stormy petrel of chess in the first decades of this century, and his system, known as hypermodern chess, revolutionized all play since his time. Casting aside the classical chess theory of Steinitz and Tarrasch, he created his own analysis of chess, considering dynamic patterns as they emerge during play. This is the fullest exposition of his ideas, and it is easily one of the dozen greatest books ever written on chess. Nimzovich illustrates each of his principles with at least two games, and shows how he applied his concepts successfully in games against such masters as Alekhine, Tarrasch, Reti, Rubinstein, Capablanca, Spielmann and others. Indispensable to every serious chess player. Translated by J. DuMont. 135 diagrams, 1 photo. xi + 364pp. 5½ x 8⅝.
T296 Paperbound **$2.25**

CHESS AND CHECKERS: THE WAY TO MASTERSHIP, Edward Lasker. Complete, lucid instructions for the beginner—and valuable suggestions for the advanced player! For both games the great master and teacher presents fundamentals, elementary tactics, and steps toward becoming a superior player. He concentrates on general principles rather than a mass of rules, comprehension rather than brute memory. Historical introduction. 118 diagrams. xiv + 167pp. 5⅜ x 8. T657 Paperbound **$1.15**

Music

A GENERAL HISTORY OF MUSIC, Charles Burney. A detailed coverage of music from the Greeks up to 1789, with full information on all types of music: sacred and secular, vocal and instrumental, operatic and symphonic. Theory, notation, forms, instruments, innovators, composers, performers, typical and important works, and much more in an easy, entertaining style. Burney covered much of Europe and spoke with hundreds of authorities and composers so that this work is more than a compilation of records . . . it is a living work of careful and first-hand scholarship. Its account of thoroughbass (18th century) Italian music is probably still the best introduction on the subject. A recent NEW YORK TIMES review said, "Surprisingly few of Burney's statements have been invalidated by modern research . . . still of great value." Edited and corrected by Frank Mercer. 35 figures. Indices. 1915pp. 5⅜ x 8. 2 volumes. **T36 The Set, Clothbound $12.50**

A DICTIONARY OF HYMNOLOGY, John Julian. This exhaustive and scholarly work has become known as an invaluable source of hundreds of thousands of important and often difficult to obtain facts on the history and use of hymns in the western world. Everyone interested in hymns will be fascinated by the accounts of famous hymns and hymn writers and amazed by the amount of practical information he will find. More than 30,000 entries on individual hymns, giving authorship, date and circumstances of composition, publication, textual variations, translations, denominational and ritual usage, etc. Biographies of more than 9,000 hymn writers, and essays on important topics such as Christmas carols and children's hymns, and much other unusual and valuable information. A 200 page double-columned index of first lines — the largest in print. Total of 1786 pages in two reinforced clothbound volumes. 6¼ x 9¼. **The set, T333 Clothbound $17.50**

MUSIC IN MEDIEVAL BRITAIN, F. Ll. Harrison. The most thorough, up-to-date, and accurate treatment of the subject ever published, beautifully illustrated. Complete account of institutions and choirs; carols, masses, and motets; liturgy and plainsong; and polyphonic music from the Norman Conquest to the Reformation. Discusses the various schools of music and their reciprocal influences; the origin and development of new ritual forms; development and use of instruments; and new evidence on many problems of the period. Reproductions of scores, over 200 excerpts from medieval melodies. Rules of harmony and dissonance; influence of Continental styles; great composers (Dunstable, Cornysh, Fairfax, etc.); and much more. Register and index of more than 400 musicians. Index of titles. General Index. 225-item bibliography. 6 Appendices. xix + 491pp. 5⅝ x 8¾. **T705 Clothbound $10.00**

THE MUSIC OF SPAIN, Gilbert Chase. Only book in English to give concise, comprehensive account of Iberian music; new Chapter covers music since 1941. Victoria, Albéniz, Cabezón, Pedrell, Turina, hundreds of other composers; popular and folk music; the Gypsies; the guitar; dance, theatre, opera, with only extensive discussion in English of the Zarzuela; virtuosi such as Casals; much more. "Distinguished . . . readable," Saturday Review. 400-item bibliography. Index. 27 photos. 383pp. 5⅜ x 8. **T549 Paperbound $2.00**

ON STUDYING SINGING, Sergius Kagen. An intelligent method of voice-training, which leads you around pitfalls that waste your time, money, and effort. Exposes rigid, mechanical systems, baseless theories, deleterious exercises. "Logical, clear, convincing . . . dead right," Virgil Thomson, N.Y. Herald Tribune. "I recommend this volume highly," Maggie Teyte, Saturday Review. 119pp. 5⅜ x 8. **T622 Paperbound $1.35**

WILLIAM LAWES, M. Lefkowitz. This is the definitive work on Lawes, the versatile, prolific, and highly original "King's musician" of 17th century England. His life is reconstructed from original documents, and nearly every piece he ever wrote is examined and evaluated: his fantasias, pavans, violin "sonatas," lyra viol and bass viol suites, and music for harp and theorbo; and his songs, masques, and theater music to words by Herrick ("Gather Ye Rosebuds"), Jonson, Suckling, Shirley, and others. The author shows the innovations of dissonance, augmented triad, and other Italian influences Lawes helped introduce to England. List of Lawes' complete works and several complete scores by this major precursor of Purcell and the 18th century developments. Index. 5 Appendices. 52 musical excerpts, many never before in print. Bibliography. x + 320pp. 5⅜ x 8. **T706 Clothbound $10.00**

THE FUGUE IN BEETHOVEN'S PIANO MUSIC, J. V. Cockshoot. The first study of a neglected aspect of Beethoven's genius: his ability as a writer of fugues. Analyses of early studies and published works demonstrate his original and powerful contributions to composition. 34 works are examined, with 143 musical excerpts. For all pianists, teachers, students, and music-minded readers with a serious interest in Beethoven. Index. 93-item bibliography. Illustration of original score for "Fugue in C." xv + 212pp. 5⅝ x 8⅜. **T704 Clothbound $6.00**

ROMAIN ROLLAND'S ESSAYS ON MUSIC, ed. by David Ewen. 16 best essays by great critic of our time, Nobel Laureate, discuss Mozart, Beethoven, Gluck, Handel, Berlioz, Wagner, Wolf, Saint-Saëns, Metastasio, Lully, Telemann, Grétry, "Origins of 18th Century 'Classic' Style," and musical life of 18th century Germany and Italy. "Shows the key to the high place that Rolland still holds in the world of music," Library Journal. 371pp. 5⅜ x 8.

T550 Paperbound **$1.50**

A GENERAL HISTORY OF THE SCIENCE AND PRACTICE OF MUSIC, Sir John Hawkins. Originally published in 1776, long regarded a genuine classic of musicology. Traces the origin and development of music theory, harmonic and contrapuntal processes, polyphony, musical notation, orchestration, instrumentation, etc. from earliest recorded evidence of music experiment to the author's own time, taking into account a score of musical forms—plainsong, motet, ballad, oratorio, opera, madrigal, canon, cantata, many more—and the particular contributions of various peoples. Still extremely valuable for its consideration of musical theorists and their work and detailed summaries and exact quotes from historically important works unavailable except in largest libraries. Biographical and critical information about hundreds of musicians undeservedly forgotten and now being rediscovered. A unique and significant work of music scholarship, prized by musicologists, composers, performers, historians of culture, and musical amateurs. Reproduction of 1853 edition. New introduction by Charles Cudworth, Curator, Pendlebury Library of Music, Cambridge, England. 315 illustrations; 60 full-page plates. 153 musical excerpts. 20 facsimiles of ancient manuscripts. Memoir of author. Index. Two volumes. Total of 1020pp. of text. 7⅞ x 10¾.

T1048-49 The set, Clothbound **$15.00**

THE GIFT TO BE SIMPLE, Edward Deming Andrews. Students of American history and culture, hymnologists, musicians, historians of religion, and anyone interested in reading about unusual peoples and customs will welcome this unique and authoritative account of Shaker music. Examines the origin of verses and of numerous Shaker dances; the rituals and gestures that accompanied singing; the unusual music theory developed by Shaker musicians and the melodies that were produced. Captures the spirit of an humble and devout people as expressed in many actual texts of hymns, dance songs, ritualistic songs, songs of humility, etc. Includes musical notations of about eighty melodies. A short introduction shows the development of the Shaker movement from its origins (about 1750), through the period of its greatest influence in the 1840's, to its post-Civil War decline. Index of first lines and melodies. Bibliography. 17 illustrations. ix + 170pp. 5⅜ x 8. T22 Paperbound **$1.50**

BEETHOVEN AND HIS NINE SYMPHONIES, George Grove, editor of Grove's Dictionary of Music and Musicians. In this modern middle-level classic of musicology Grove not only analyzes all nine of Beethoven's symphonies very thoroughly in terms of their musical structure, but also discusses the circumstances under which they were written, Beethoven's stylistic development, and much other background material. This is an extremely rich book, yet very easily followed; it is highly recommended to anyone seriously interested in music. Over 250 musical passages. Index. viii + 407pp. 5⅜ x 8. T334 Paperbound **$2.00**

AIDA BY GIUSEPPI VERDI, translated and introduced by Ellen H. Bleiler. Full handbook to the most popular opera of all; everything the operagoer (or listener) needs except the music itself. Complete Italian libretto, with all repeats, with new, modern English translation in parallel columns; biography of Verdi and librettists; background to composition of Aida; musical history; plot summary; musical excerpts; pictorial section of 76 illustrations showing Verdi, famous singers, famous performances, etc. Large clear type for easy reading. 147pp. 5⅝ x 8½. T405 Paperbound **$1.00**

LA BOHEME BY GIACOMO PUCCINI, translated and introduced by Ellen H. Bleiler. Complete handbook for the operagoer, with everything needed for full enjoyment except the musical score itself. Complete Italian libretto, with new modern English line-by-line translation—the only libretto printing all repeats; biography of Puccini; the librettists; background to the opera, Murger's La Boheme, etc.; circumstances of composition and performances; plot summary; and pictorial section of 73 illustrations showing Puccini, famous singers and performances, etc. Large clear type for easy reading. 124pp. 5⅜ x 8½. T404 Paperbound **$1.00**

Prices subject to change without notice.

Dover publishes books on art, music, philosophy, literature, languages, history, social sciences, psychology, handcrafts, orientalia, puzzles and entertainments, chess, pets and gardens, books explaining science, intermediate and higher mathematics, mathematical physics, engineering, biological sciences, earth sciences, classics of science, etc. Write to:

Dept. catrr.
Dover Publications, Inc.
180 Varick Street, N.Y. 14, N.Y.